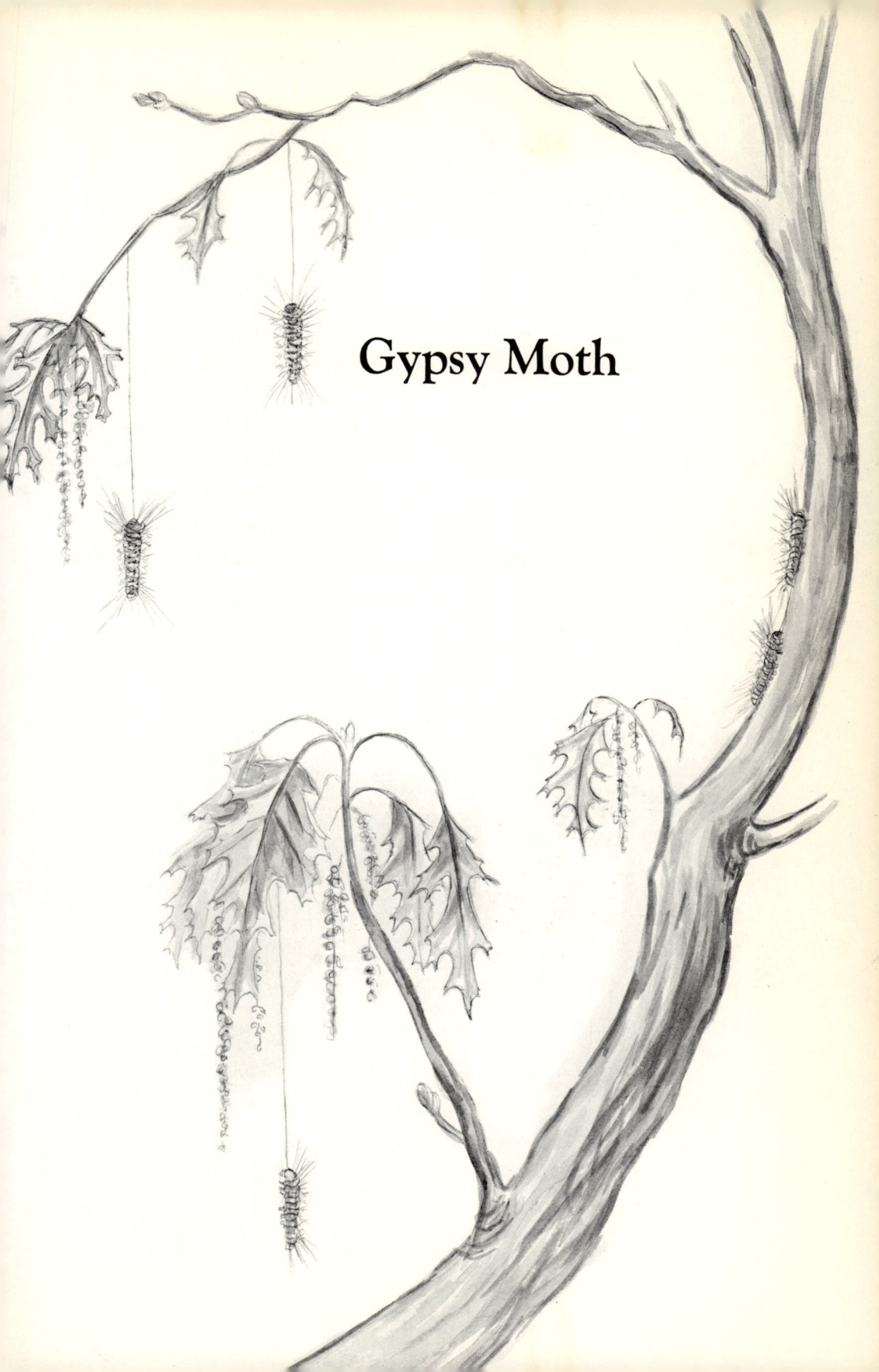

Gypsy Moth

BY THE SAME AUTHOR

Lost Wild America,
the Story of Our Extinct and Vanishing Wildlife
Mice, Moose, and Men,
How Their Populations Rise and Fall
Moths and Butterflies and How They Live
Bees, Wasps, and Hornets and How They Live
Aquatic Insects and How They Live

Gypsy Moth
ITS HISTORY IN AMERICA

Written and Illustrated by
Robert M. McClung

William Morrow and Company
New York 1974

Acknowledgments

In doing research and gathering material for this book, the author was helped by the generosity of a number of organizations and individuals who forwarded material, patiently answered questions, and offered advice. I gratefully acknowledge my indebtedness to all of them.

Officials of the Forest Service, United States Department of Agriculture, and representatives of the Departments of Agriculture, Forestry, or Conservation in a number of states supplied very helpful material. So did the Gypsy Moth Advisory Council and the Massachusetts Audubon Society. The staff of the Gypsy Moth Methods Improvement Laboratory on Cape Cod—especially Mr. John Secrest and Mr. Winfred McLane—were very helpful and hospitable.

Particular thanks are due to Mr. Philip Dowden, United States Department of Agriculture (retired); Dr. Stephen Collins, Professor of Biological Sciences at Southern Connecticut State College; and to Dr. Robert B. Whitney, Professor Emeritus of Chemistry at Amherst College, and to Mrs. Whitney. All of them read and criticized the entire manuscript and offered many helpful suggestions. All statements and opinions expressed in the book, however, are the sole responsibility of the author.

Illustrations on pages 25, 27, 28, and 30 are based on period photographs, and map on page 33 is adapted from maps prepared by the Massachusetts State Board of Agriculture. Maps on pages 38 and 83 are based on USDA maps and other data.

Copyright © 1974 by Robert M. McClung

All rights reserved. No part of this book may be reproduced or utilized in any form or by any means, electronic or mechanical, including photocopying, recording or by any information storage and retrieval system, without permission in writing from the Publisher. Inquiries should be addressed to William Morrow and Company, Inc., 105 Madison Ave., New York, N.Y. 10016.
Printed in the United States of America.
1   2   3   4   5   78   77   76   75   74

Library of Congress Cataloging in Publication Data
McClung, Robert M
   Gypsy moth: its history in America.
   SUMMARY: Describes the life cycle of the gypsy moth and man's attempts to control this insect's often damaging effects on trees and forests.
   Bibliography: p.
   1. Gipsy-moth—United States—Juvenile literature. 2. Gipsy-moth—Control—United States—Juvenile literature. [1. Gypsy moth. 2. Pest control] I. Title.
SB945.G9M29   632'.7'81   74-6245
ISBN 0-688-20124-5
ISBN 0-688-30124-X (lib. bdg.)

Contents

I. **Life Cycle of the Gypsy Moth 7**
A Female Moth Emerges / The Male's Antennae / Gypsy Lays Her Eggs / What the Caterpillars Eat / Molting and Growing / The Pupa / An Outbreak of Gypsy Moths

II. **The Invasion of America 19**
The Experiments of Monsieur Trouvelot / Some Caterpillars Escape / A Plague of Caterpillars / How People Fought the Invasion / Mechanical Methods of Control / Early Chemical Warfare / State Funds Cut Off

III. **Gypsy Moth Spreads 32**
A Program of Reasonable Control / Insect Enemies from the Old World / Barrier Zone Established / The Hurricane of 1938

IV. **Chemical Warfare 40**
The Use of DDT / The Air Age in Insect Control / Trapping Male Moths / Intensive Spraying of 1957 / Harmful Effects of DDT / DDT Dies Hard / Other Chemicals Used / Testing New Insecticides in the Field

V. **Biological Controls 57**
Natural Balance / Insect Parasites and Predators / Viral

and Bacterial Infections / Scent Traps / Insect Sterilization / The Juvenile Hormone / Rivers of Natural Insecticides / Insect Repellents / Raising Caterpillars for Research

VI. Prescription Entomology 77
Integrated Pest Control / Enforcing the Quarantine / Opposing Points of View / The Problem

Appendix: 86
Insect Pests Often Mistaken for Gypsy Moths

Further Reading 90

Index 93

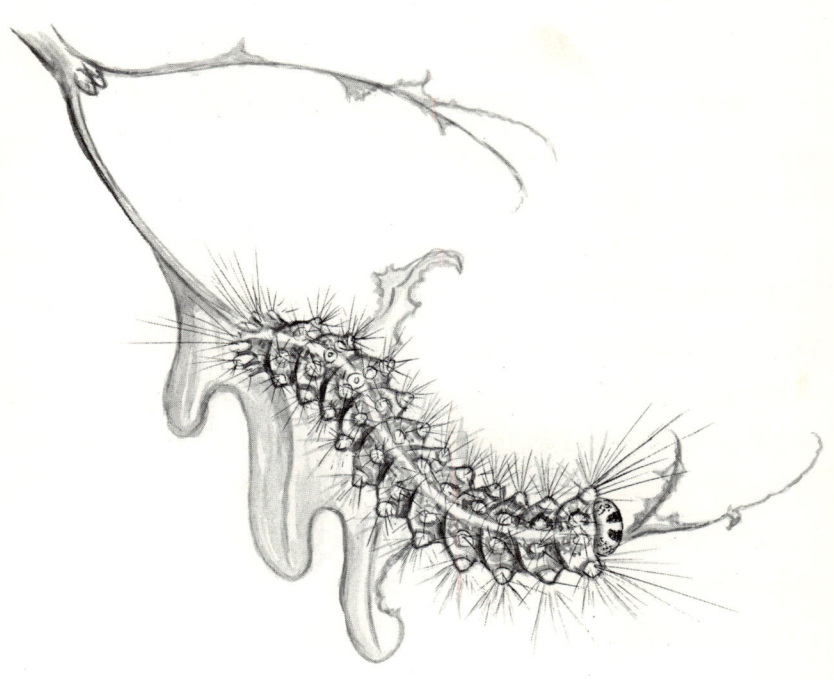

I
Life Cycle of the Gypsy Moth

"One of the greatest insect pests in history." Or, "Public enemy number one in our woodlands!" Such statements are typical of the way some people speak of the gypsy moth. Others say that while it may sometimes be a nuisance, it does little real damage to woodlands at all.

Both groups would agree, however, that the gypsy moth worries the general public greatly. Along with the field mouse, the prairie dog, the wolf, and many other wild creatures, this insect has the habit of consuming food or other materials that man wants for his own use.

A native of Europe, Asia, and northern Africa, the gypsy moth (*Porthetria dispar*) is harmless as an adult. It is as a leaf-eating caterpillar that gypsy does all of its damage. When it reaches full growth, the caterpillar spins a flimsy cocoon—really no more than a network of a few silken threads. Hundreds of other kinds of caterpillars spin silk shelters that are far superior. Yet the gypsy moth was first brought to the United States for some misguided experiments in silk production.

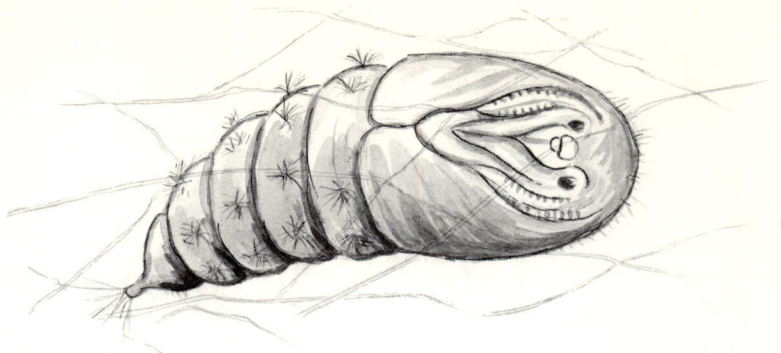

Unfortunately, some of those caterpillars escaped from captivity in 1869. In the century since, the gypsy moth has repeatedly stripped the leaves from millions of acres of woodland in the northeastern United States. Many millions of dollars have been spent in efforts to exterminate or control the species. Yet, in spite of all these campaigns, the gypsy moth has flourished and spread as generation has succeeded generation.

A Female Moth Emerges

In a New England woodlot, gypsy moth pupae lie in their silken hammocks like tiny brown mummies. One particularly fat pupa twists and turns in its flimsy cocoon located in a fold of bark near the base of an oak tree. The time is early August, and the adult insect within the pupa is ready to emerge. Pushing against the brown pupal walls, the female moth finally breaks the protective case,

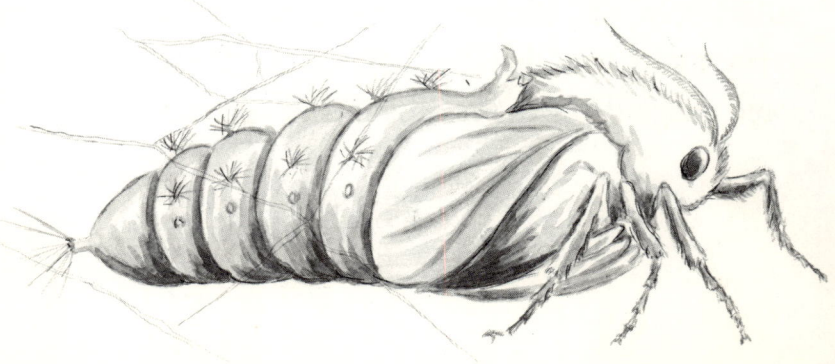

and her head and waving legs appear. Then the back of the pupal skin cracks open, and within a few seconds she crawls free.

Wet and bedraggled, with tiny flaplike wings, the moth scrambles a few steps over the rough bark and searches for a suitable perch. Soon she rests quietly while her wings begin to expand and dry. Pumping her abdomen, she forces fluid and air into the veins in her wings. Limp as cloth at first, the wings gradually expand, then stiffen and dry. They are white with narrow black markings and lie folded over her body like a tent. Spread wide, they would measure two and a half inches from tip to tip. But gypsy's wings are useless, for her plump body is full of eggs and so heavy that she cannot fly. She has no need for flight, however. She is ready to mate almost as soon as she emerges from her cocoon, and she is able to lure male moths to her.

Thrusting out her sex organ from the tip of her abdomen, the female gypsy releases a powerful perfume from scent glands on either side of it. The afternoon breeze carries this scent far and wide. Male moths as much as a half mile or more downwind are able to pick up the scent and fly toward it.

The Male's Antennae

Smaller than the female, the male gypsy moth has dusky brown wings. Unlike most moths, he flies by day—usually from midmorning until midafternoon. He is an active and rapid flier, a difficult target for birds or other enemies as he flutters back and forth, following the scent trail to his prospective mate. Because of his erratic flight, the French know him as *le zigzag*. His dusky color may have inspired his common English name, *gypsy*. Or perhaps it comes from the moth's unpredictable appearances throughout its range over many countries of the Old World. The fact that the male and female moths look quite different accounts for the moth's specific scientific name, *dispar*. It comes from a Latin word meaning *different,* or *unlike*.

The male moth's body is slender and streamlined, and he has wide plumed antennae that look like little feathers. These antennae bear countless tiny sensors that enable him to pick up the female scent and find his way to her.

Closer and closer to the female he flies. At last he locates her and flutters wildly about her. In a moment he mates with her, and the two remain together for several hours, resting quietly on the tree trunk.

Gypsy Lays Her Eggs

Soon after they separate, the female begins to lay her round yellow eggs, usually some 300 to 500 of them. A particularly big female may lay 1000 eggs or more. Once she has finished, she dies within a few days.

The eggs are all deposited in one big cluster, usually within a few inches of the spot where the female emerged from the pupa and mated. Stuck to the bark and to each other with a varnishlike substance, the eggs are hidden under a protective layer of brown hairlike scales from the female's abdomen. Covered with this felt blanket, the inch-and-a-half-long egg mass looks like a brown cocoon.

The gypsy eggs are laid in midsummer, but they do not hatch until the following spring. During the warm fall days, however, a tiny caterpillar quickly develops inside each egg. It remains curled up in the shell throughout the fall and winter, as if hibernating.

Springtime comes, and the days grow longer and warmer. In late April and early May the leaves begin to

sprout on the trees. Now each tiny caterpillar finally chews an opening ring around its eggshell and emerges. About an eighth of an inch long, it is dark-colored and bristles with tufts of hair.

For a day or two after they hatch, the caterpillars huddle on the egg cluster, especially if the weather is cold or rainy. But when the sun comes out, they start to travel. Climbing up the tree trunk and onto the branches, they begin to eat leaves.

At this time, when they are just several days old, the larvae sometimes suspend themselves on silken threads from the branches. The fragile threads often break, and rising air currents carry the tiny hairy caterpillars upward. At this stage the larvae have many special hairs with inflated globules—like tiny balloons—near their bases. These hairs help to make the little caterpillars extremely light. Sailing far and wide on the breezes, they finally drop into new territory, sometimes many miles from where they took off.

larval hair, showing inflated globule near base

What the Caterpillars Eat

Gypsy caterpillars eat the leaves of a great number of different kinds of trees and plants. Oaks are preferred, but willow, birch, and many fruit trees are also favored. When they are not available, the larger caterpillars will eat practically any kind of leaves around them, including the needles of pine, hemlock, and other evergreens. Only a handful of trees—ash, sycamore, and tulip poplar among them— seem to be immune from attack.

When the gypsy moth invades new territory, it is often at its most destructive for several years before its population drops. If trees are stripped of their leaves two or three times in succession over a period of several years, many of them will be seriously weakened, and therefore more susceptible to drought or disease. Some of them will die. Pines frequently die after just one complete defoliation, and hemlocks almost always do. The gypsy-moth population usually falls, however, before great damage is done to the woodland.

By the time a caterpillar is full grown, it may eat as much as eleven or twelve square inches of leaf surface every day. Under usual conditions, it feeds mostly at night and is especially active from dusk until three or four in the morning. When the summer dawn is about to break, it stops eating and crawls down the tree trunk to find a hiding place. It rests during the day, often in company with hundreds of its brothers and sisters, under loose pieces of bark, in tree holes, under debris, or in

This caterpillar has just molted. Note the discarded head shell.

other sheltered and shady areas. When there is a heavy infestation of caterpillars, however, many of them do not get enough to eat during the night and so continue to feed during the day.

Molting and Growing

The caterpillar eats and eats and grows and grows as the days go by. When its skin becomes too tight, the larva sheds it for a newer, looser skin that has developed beneath the old one. Before it pupates, a male caterpillar usually molts its skin five times, and the female caterpillar six times.

Just after it has shed its skin, the caterpillar's head is very big in proportion to its body. The head has a hard shell-like covering and will not increase in size until the next molt. The caterpillar's body, however, is enclosed by a soft wrinkled skin that stretches out as the larva grows.

After each molt, the caterpillar looks somewhat different from the way it looked before. Each of these distinctive stages of growth between molts is known as an *instar*. When it is full grown, in the fifth or sixth instar, the gypsy caterpillar is a very handsome creature. Its skin

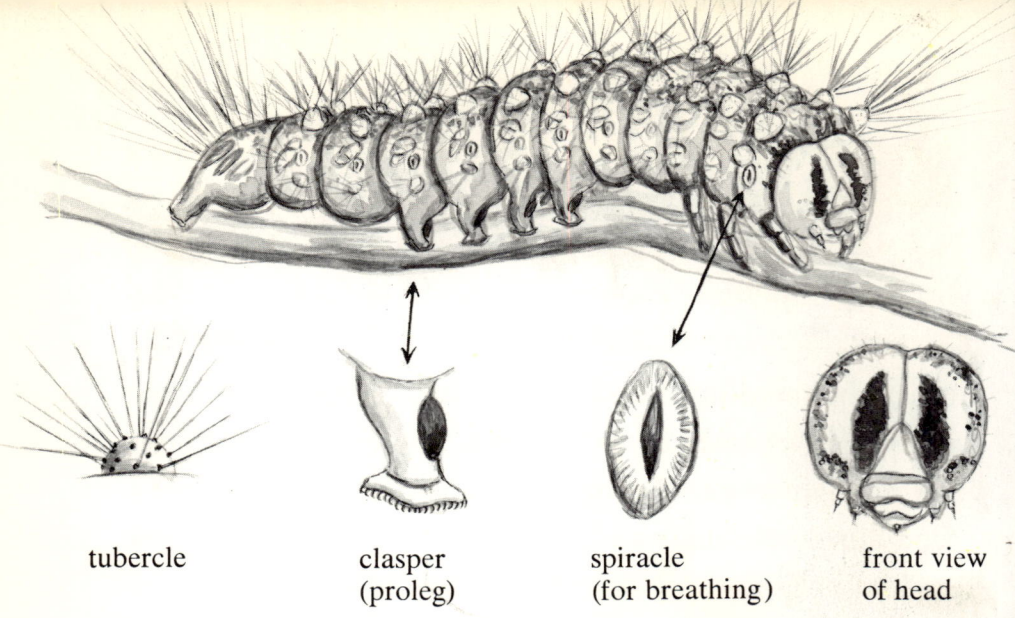

| tubercle | clasper (proleg) | spiracle (for breathing) | front view of head |

is mostly a creamy yellow color with many irregular black markings. A broad yellow line runs down the caterpillar's back. On either side of this line are a row of warty knobs, or tubercles, bright blue on the first five body segments, brilliant red on the last six. Below them, on either side, the caterpillar has another row of big yellowish knobs. All of the tubercles are topped by bristly tufts of long black or straw-colored hairs.

On the sixth and seventh body segments are two red mounds—glands filled with a scented liquid. Some observers suspect that this liquid may have a disagreeable smell or taste that helps to protect the caterpillar.

The Pupa

Full grown after seven to ten weeks, the caterpillar seeks out some sheltered spot where it rests quietly for a day or two before starting to spin its cocoon. Finally it anchors a few long strands of silk to the bark or other base as a framework. Then it spins a number of short strands across and between the longer ones. When it is finished, the flimsy cocoon is little more than a thin network of silk surrounding the caterpillar.

The caterpillar hunches up, and its body seems to shrivel. It looks dead, but it isn't. After several days the caterpillar's skin splits down the back once again, and the pupa that has been forming beneath begins to work its way out. Pushing with many tiny hooks at the tip of its abdomen, the pupa gradually squirms its way clear of the crumpled caterpillar skin and lies free. Soft and green at first, the pupa quickly hardens and darkens to a shiny mahogany color.

After ten to fifteen days, the adult moth that has been developing within the pupa is ready to emerge. Splitting the tough brown shell, the moth crawls free. Within an

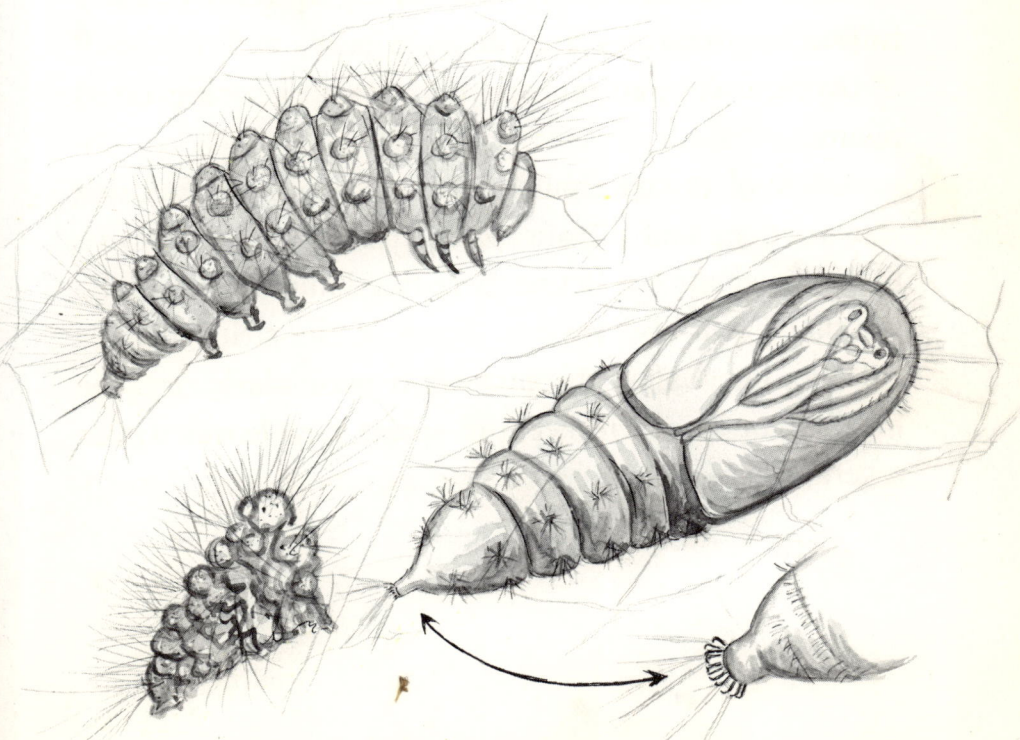

hour or two, the female moth often begins to send out her sex lure. The cycle is repeating itself once again. Next year there may be more caterpillars in the woods than there were this year. If conditions are especially favorable, there may be a population explosion of gypsy moths.

An Outbreak of Gypsy Moths

Imagine walking through a woodland in early July, after such an outbreak has occurred. The trees, instead of showing normal midsummer greenery, appear bare and lifeless, their naked branches sharply outlined against the sky. The whole area looks as if a forest fire had just swept through it; or as it might appear in late November, after most of the leaves had fallen, except that there is no thick carpet of fallen leaves.

Starving caterpillars still roam the forest floor, vainly searching for food. The bases of the trees are surrounded by larvae that are either dead or dying from diseases caused by overcrowding. The air is heavy with the smell of drying leaf fragments and the stench of rotting caterpillars.

A few of the caterpillars are still healthy. They will spin cocoons and pupate. The gypsy moth will survive in the woodland but in greatly reduced numbers. And the woodland will also survive. Some of the stripped trees will die; but, unless the summer is particularly dry, the majority of them will begin to sprout new leaves within several weeks.

II
The Invasion of America

Throughout its natural Old World range, the gypsy moth has long been recognized as a serious tree pest. Indeed, its generic name, *Porthetria,* comes from a Greek word meaning *to ravage,* or *lay waste.* Eyewitness accounts from many countries tell of outbreaks during which vast armies of caterpillars stripped woodlands of their leaves and left orchards and shade trees bare and desolate. Hordes of gypsy caterpillars have more than once played havoc with the valuable cork trees of France and with Berlin's famous linden trees. Many forests all over Europe have been ravaged repeatedly.

One old account relates how "Some of the common people thought that the caterpillars grew out of the ground, like the grass; others thought they were created by the evil one; still others assured the author that they had seen with their own eyes thousands of caterpillars brought with the wind; and finally, there were many who thought that these caterpillars were sent by God as a punishment of their sins."

The Experiments of Monsieur Trouvelot

In spite of such accounts, a French scientist, Monsieur Leopold Trouvelot, had some gypsy-moth eggs sent to him in the United States, where he was working during the 1860's. He wanted them so that he could conduct various silk-raising experiments with the caterpillars. A versatile naturalist and artist, Monsieur Trouvelot was also an astronomer and worked at the Harvard Observatory in Cambridge, Massachusetts. Instead of living in Cambridge, however, he had settled in Medford, a quiet village about five miles to the north.

In this rural atmosphere Trouvelot carried on his extensive experiments with various kinds of caterpillars. It was rumored that he wanted to breed hybrid silkworms that would be hardier than the Chinese species and that could be used to establish a silk industry in the United States. In the course of his work, Trouvelot tested the quality of the silk produced by the caterpillars of various American moths, especially the Polyphemus. This species is a large and beautiful moth whose larva spins a stout oval cocoon of glistening white silk.

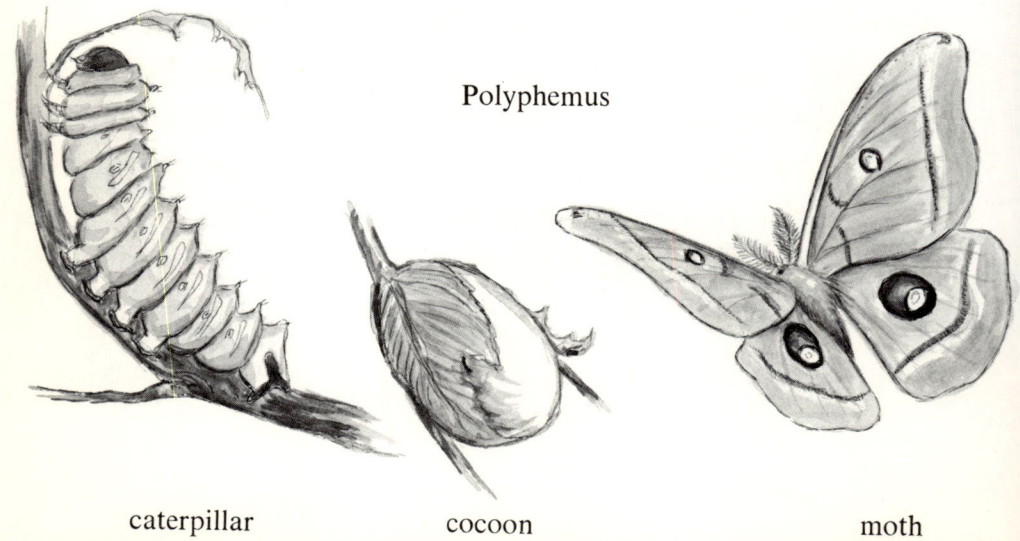

Polyphemus

caterpillar   cocoon   moth

In one account of his experiments, Trouvelot complained that birds were eating many of his caterpillars. To prevent such losses, he enclosed a five-acre woodlot with an eight-foot fence, and then stretched netting over many small trees and branches within the area. He placed his caterpillars on these protected branches after they had hatched from eggs that he kept in jars inside the house. By 1865 he claimed to have a million caterpillars all feeding under protective netting. His five acres of woodland, he noted with considerable satisfaction, ". . . were swarming with caterpillar life."

With his knowledge of insects, Trouvelot was certainly aware that the gypsy caterpillar—a common species in his native France—spins a very inferior cocoon, hardly more than a loose network of threads. Nonetheless, he wanted to work with them. He undoubtedly received them in the form of egg clusters, which could be sent across the ocean safely and easily during the winter season.

Some Caterpillars Escape

Accounts vary as to how the gypsy moths or their caterpillars escaped. Some say that a jar containing eggs or newly hatched larvae was placed near an open window in 1869, and then broken during a windstorm, scattering the contents. Others say that the flimsy netting enclosing the caterpillars outside was ripped open during a summer storm. Perhaps both events occurred.

When Trouvelot discovered what had happened, he searched for the missing specimens and gathered up as many of them as he could. But some, he realized, were still at large. The loss troubled him, for he well knew what damage the gypsy moth sometimes inflicted in Europe. He could only guess what it might do in the United States, where it did not have the same natural enemies to help control its population.

Under the circumstances, he did the best he could and had notices published in various scientific journals warning of the escape. But no one seemed particularly concerned. In time, Monsieur Trouvelot returned to his native France, and for some years very little was heard or noted about the escaped caterpillars or their descendants. But they survived in Medford, and as the years went by their numbers increased.

A Plague of Caterpillars

By 1881, gypsy caterpillars had become so common in the neighborhood of Trouvelot's old home in Medford that the villagers considered them a local nuisance. The caterpillars were just one more insect pest with which they had to cope, although the exact species was still unknown to them.

Then the population of gypsy caterpillars exploded during the spring of 1889. The year before had been a good one for insects, and gypsy moths had flourished and laid record numbers of eggs. When warm weather arrived in the spring of 1889, it brought with it a shattering increase of gypsy caterpillars.

Hatching out by the millions that April and May, gypsy caterpillars chewed up leaves and grew and marched in vast armies from one devastated yard in Medford to another. Stripping every leaf from the trees in one area, they crawled down the trunks in solid masses and moved across a yard or street to attack the vegetation there. Everywhere a person walked he stepped on caterpillars or slipped on their crushed bodies. Caterpillars covered tree trunks, fences, and sides of houses.

One distressed citizen, Mr. J. P. Dill, lamented that ". . . there was not a place on the outside of the house where you could put your hand without touching caterpillars. . . . If we walked under the trees we got nothing less than a shower bath of caterpillars. . . . The caterpillars were so thick on the trees that they stuck together like cold macaroni. A little later in the season we saw literally thousands of moths fluttering in the backyard."

Another, Mr. D. W. Daley, said, "At night we could hear the caterpillars eating in the trees and their excrement dropping to the ground. . . ."

Dr. C. H. Fernald, Professor of Entomology at Massachusetts Agricultural College in Amherst, came to view the desolation after his return from a European trip. His son, Dr. H. T. Fernald, had already identified the culprits as gypsy-moth caterpillars native to Europe. Professor Fernald immediately urged the State Legislature to appropriate funds to fight the moth and wipe it out before it spread any further.

How People Fought the Invasion

In the meantime, desperate property owners fought the hordes of invading caterpillars in every way they could. Many people spent a great deal of their time that summer sweeping masses of caterpillars from tree trunks, sidewalks, and the sides of houses and sheds. They collected them by the bucketful and killed them with boiling water. They swept caterpillars into great piles, like leaves, in their yards, then doused them with kerosene and set fire to them.

The damage—both real and imagined—was so great that the Massachusetts Legislature finally took Professor Fernald's advice and appropriated $50,000 to be used for combating the pest. A Gypsy Moth Commission was created under the State Board of Agriculture, and Edward H. Forbush, an energetic young ornithologist, was appointed its director, in charge of waging the campaign against the moth.

As soon as money was available that spring of 1890, a crew of workers began a systematic program of searching for egg masses and destroying them. In May, after caterpillars had hatched, a program of spraying infested trees with Paris green, an arsenic poison, was started.

workmen using cyclone burner to destroy egg masses

In addition, special guards were employed to inspect wagons, carriages, and buggies as they passed designated checkpoints and to remove any caterpillars, moths, or egg clusters that they found. Such procedures, it was figured, would help to prevent the moth's spread.

In the spring of 1891, the Gypsy Moth Commission held a conference to which they invited many prominent entomologists from all over the country. They asked these men to assess the work done so far and to tell them what they thought should be done in the future. Some of the delegates urged an all-out, one-year campaign of extermination. "Wipe out the gypsy moth!" was their cry. Others suggested that the moth could be controlled by paying school children to gather its egg masses. Still others claimed that spraying was the best method of control.

As a result of these widely varying proposals, a comprehensive plan of attack was drawn up and put into effect for the next ten years. Its ultimate aim was the extermination of the moth in the United States.

Mechanical Methods of Control

Armies of workers were kept busy scraping egg clusters from trees and destroying them. Another method was to kill them where they were by covering them with creosote or coal tar. In the first six weeks of 1891, some 750,000 egg clusters were gotten rid of in this manner. Work crews sometimes climbed to the tops of the highest trees to search for eggs, and one year the gigantic Dexter elm—a famous 110-foot monarch located in the town of Malden—was cleared by this method.

Gathering places for caterpillars were created by tying strips of burlap around tree trunks. Seeking daytime shelters, the caterpillars would group under these artificial hiding places. There they could be collected easily and killed by attendants who checked the burlap bands daily. More than 600,000 trees were burlapped in this way in 1894, and untold millions of caterpillars were destroyed by some 265 workers.

Bands of tanglefoot, or caterpillar glue, were placed around the trunks of many trees to protect them. Tanglefoot is a sticky substance that has a repellent effect and prevents many caterpillars from crawling up the trunk. Some try to cross it, however, and become stuck. Sometimes so many caterpillars become entrapped that they form a bridge over which other caterpillars crawl to the branches above.

In addition, many badly infested areas of woodland and brush were cut and burned. Tree holes and other

workman placing burlap on trees

likely hiding places for the caterpillars were filled with cement. Decaying branches were pruned. In the year 1899 alone, some 17 million trees were inspected. Of them, 2,304,552 were banded and burlapped, and in very heavily infested areas, in a desperate attempt to curb the outbreak, 468,790 were cut down.

Early Chemical Warfare

Insecticides were used against the caterpillars, too. Trees were usually sprayed with arsenate of lead or Paris green—both of them highly poisonous arsenic compounds. When applied correctly—as much as 30 pounds per 150 gallons of water was sometimes recommended—arsenate of lead usually did not injure trees or "burn" the foliage. The mixture stuck well to the leaves, and sometimes only one spraying a season was needed. On the other hand, the mixture could poison any man or beast that came in contact with it.

Paris green was usually mixed at the rate of one pound per 150 gallons of water. It was not as persistent on foliage as arsenate of lead, and several sprayings a season were usually needed to be effective. Furthermore, Paris green also roused fears of arsenic poisoning. The danger to people, farm animals, and water supplies was widely discussed.

Some people became so incensed at the spray programs of the 1890's that they held public meetings to oppose them. One newspaper advised property owners to "shoot

on sight" the workmen engaged in spraying. This spraying was usually done by automatic sprayers that were horse drawn or by even smaller units that two men could manipulate and power with a hand pump.

State Funds Cut Off

The combined methods kept the gypsy moth under control quite well during the 1890's, and even wiped it out in many areas. The main trouble was, the Gypsy Moth Commission grumbled, that they usually ran out of money every year just when they needed to hire winter crews. These crews were sent out to gather and destroy the egg clusters before they hatched. Every year the State Legislature tended to appropriate the needed funds tardily.

In spite of such frustrations, the Commission did its work so well that by the spring of 1900 the moth no longer seemed to be a major threat within the state. Its range had been pushed back in many areas, and all the principal infestations were under control. Professor Fernald, the Amherst entomologist, confidently stated that the moth could be completely exterminated in the United States within fifteen years, provided at least $200,000 a year was supplied for the first five years, $100,000 a year for the second five years, and $15,000 a year for the third five years.

A special investigating committee of the State Legislature saw the matter in a somewhat different light. The gypsy-moth campaign had gone so well, they argued, that now there was no need to appropriate more money. There were no severe outbreaks, they declared, and ". . . it is fighting against the laws of nature to attempt extermination." All that was needed was suppression, and the gypsy moth had already been suppressed.

As a result of these views, the State Legislature decided not to appropriate any funds at all for gypsy-moth control in 1900. Individual towns would be responsible, it decided, for combating local infestations within their boundaries.

The Gypsy Moth Commission and the State Board of Agriculture were furious at this decision. "Suppression," they declared, "is gradual expansion." The gypsy moth would soon be more plentiful than ever, they predicted, and all their hard work of the previous ten years would go for nothing.

III
Gypsy Moth Spreads

Events soon proved the Commission right. Extermination had been a distinct possibility when the gypsy moth's population was restricted to a small area. But without any coordinated attempt to control the moth, it multiplied rapidly during the next several years and extended its range into a number of new areas in Massachusetts. Then, in 1901, colonies of gypsy caterpillars were discovered in Providence, Rhode Island. The Massachusetts Board of Agriculture claimed that "Every circumstance yet discovered indicates that the moth was deliberately taken to Providence and purposely scattered by some malicious or irresponsible person."

By 1904, the moth had become so abundant once again in Massachusetts that a number of local associations were formed to fight it. These groups soon banded together to form the Massachusetts Association for the Suppression of the Gypsy and Brown-tail Moth. The latter was another unwanted foreigner that had found its way from Europe to the Boston area in the 1890's.

By 1905, more than 120 cities and towns in Massachusetts reported infestations of gypsy moths. In five years the range of the pest had increased from 359 to 2224 square miles—about a quarter of the State's area. By this time it had also invaded New Hampshire.

A Program of Reasonable Control

The *Medford Mercury,* newspaper of the town where the gypsy moth had first appeared, was particularly alarmed. "At times whole regiments of the German Army have been set to work in the forests destroying the caterpillars," the newspaper declared, "and it is apparent that the scourge in America will exceed the European ravages unless its growth is speedily checked."

As if in answer, the Massachusetts Legislature reversed its position of five years before and passed An Act to Provide for the Suppression of the Gypsy and Brown-tail Moths. This act required that local communities fight the moths within their limits and provided

Gypsy Moth Spread, 1869-1908, Massachusetts

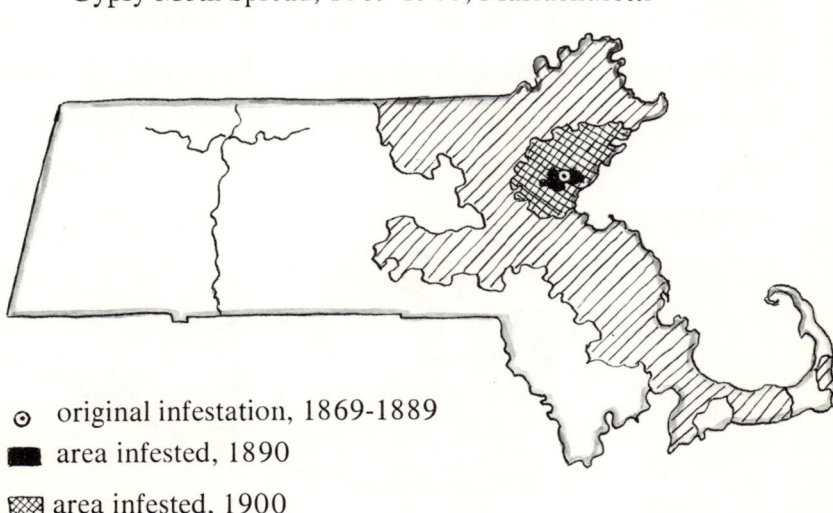

- ⊙ original infestation, 1869-1889
- ■ area infested, 1890
- ▨ area infested, 1900
- ▨ area infested, 1908

State funds to help. The governor promptly appointed Mr. A. H. Kirkland, an assistant of Forbush on the original commission, as Superintendent for Suppressing the Gypsy and Brown-tail Moths.

Mr. Kirkland's philosophy as he took over was reasonable control of the moths. "Time when either pest could have been exterminated has long since passed," he admitted. He had the authority to order various towns to spend funds as needed for gypsy-moth control, and the State promised $300,000 over the next three years to help carry out the new program. It would, in addition, appropriate $10,000 yearly for research on the moth's natural enemies.

Insect Enemies from the Old World

During the 1890's, when extermination of the gypsy moth had been the aim, little attention had been paid to the idea of establishing any of the species' Old World enemies in the United States. If the moth were eliminated completely, then there would be no need to import any of them.

Once the decision was made to control the gypsy moth rather than try to exterminate it, however, the use of

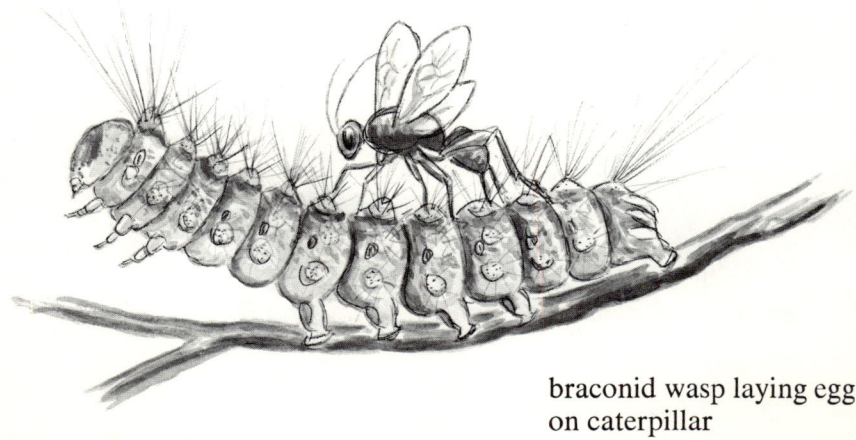

braconid wasp laying egg on caterpillar

insect parasites and predators as allies became a serious consideration. In 1905, Professor L. O. Howard, Chief of the Bureau of Entomology of the United States Department of Agriculture, visited Europe in order to study these natural enemies of the gypsy moth and make arrangements for shipping some of them to the United States. The next year Congress voted funds to help the campaign to suppress the gypsy moth, and the Department of Agriculture has been involved ever since.

Until 1905, the State of Massachusetts had maintained a small laboratory in the town of Malden for research on gypsy moths and their insect enemies. In 1905, this research was moved to Saugus, and two years later to a special parasite laboratory, which had been established in Melrose.

Through Professor Howard's efforts, nearly 200,000 gypsy-moth caterpillars, which were thought to be infected with parasites, were shipped to the laboratories from Europe and Japan in 1907. The parasitic insects included various species of wasps and flies that laid their eggs in or on the eggs, larvae, or pupae of gypsy moths. After hatching, the parasitic larvae would feed on their hosts and kill them.

A European caterpillar-hunting beetle proved to be another effective enemy. Great numbers of this beetle, as well as parasitic wasps and flies, were reared at the laboratories and released to join in the fight against the gypsy moth.

An active program of importing, raising, and releasing gypsy-moth parasites was conducted by the United States Department of Agriculture from 1907 until 1914, when it was interrupted by the First World War. The importation of parasites was renewed in 1921 and continued until 1931, when it was replaced by a program of rearing and distributing various species that were already established in this country.

Barrier Zone Established

Mr. Kirkland carried on an energetic program of gypsy-moth suppression in Massachusetts, using every method that had proved successful before, as well as trying out a few new techniques and products.

One of these products was a new commercial preparation said to be very useful for banding tree trunks and preventing caterpillars from climbing into the foliage. Named Razzle-Dazzle, it stopped the caterpillars fairly effectively, Kirkland noted, but it had a serious drawback: it was so powerful that it stopped the flow of sap in the tree trunk, thus girdling the tree and killing it outright.

In 1912, the Federal Government passed a Quarantine Act and established a system of inspecting trees and other live plant material shipped from infested areas to uninfested areas. Automobiles were just coming into common use, it was noted, and they were an additional vehicle for spreading the moth into new territory.

In spite of every effort, the gypsy moth continued to widen its range, heading westward at the rate of six miles every year. By 1920, it was securely established in all of the New England states. That same year New Jersey reported a sizable colony of the moths near Somerville. This new outbreak had evidently resulted from the importation a few years before of a number of infested blue spruce trees from Holland. Both the State of New Jersey and the United States Department of Agriculture began a vigorous campaign against the species in this new area. After fifteen years of effort and untold expenditures, they claimed that the moth had been completely stamped out in New Jersey.

In the meantime, the gypsy moth was spreading into other areas at such an alarming rate that the Department of Agriculture in 1923 instituted a new control concept. It involved the establishment of a barrier zone many miles wide, stretching from the Canadian border down the Hudson River valley and ending on Long Island. Particularly vigorous methods were to be used within this barrier zone to search out and clean up local infestations of the moth, thus preventing its further spread westward and southward. Any colonies discovered outside the barrier zone were to be eradicated completely.

The Hurricane of 1938

In 1932, a thriving colony of gypsy moths was discovered near Wilkes-Barre, Pennsylvania, a location clearly outside the barrier zone. It was a well-established population, obviously several years old. In spite of every effort to prevent its spread, the moth had managed to breach the barrier zone and become established on the other side.

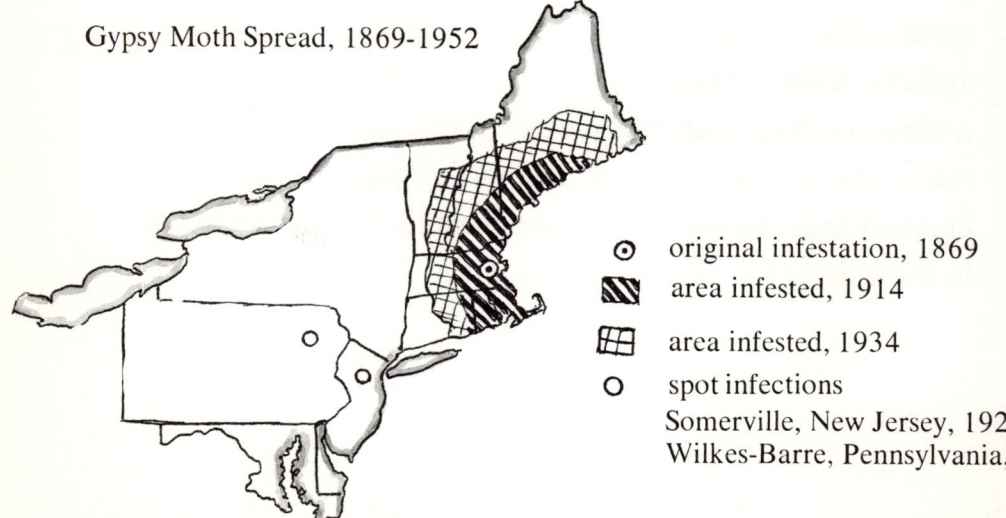

Gypsy Moth Spread, 1869-1952

⊙ original infestation, 1869
▨ area infested, 1914
▦ area infested, 1934
○ spot infections
   Somerville, New Jersey, 1920
   Wilkes-Barre, Pennsylvania, 1

Six years later a violent hurricane swept northward through New England in September, 1938. Several years afterward the gypsy moth was discovered in Ohio, and many people blamed the hurricane's winds for carrying the moth far west of its Pennsylvania and New York range. In September—the time of the hurricane—however, the only living stage of the gypsy moth is the egg mass, which is usually firmly attached to a tree trunk or branch. Perhaps rivers swollen to flood stage by the storm's rains had swept uprooted trees or broken branches infested with egg clusters into new areas. Whatever had happened, the gypsy moth had spread its range once again, despite all the efforts being made to control it.

A year after the hurricane the Second World War began. With the war came a new insecticide that was hailed as the ultimate weapon for stamping out insect pests everywhere. That insecticide was DDT.

IV
Chemical Warfare

Seeking new poisons for chemical warfare during the 1930's, research chemists developed a series of deadly new compounds—the synthetic organic poisons. They are synthetic, because they do not occur naturally in nature and are created artificially in the laboratory. They are organic, because they are formed by manipulating carbon, one of the "basic building blocks of life."

One group of these newly discovered compounds was the organic phosphates, such as malathion and parathion. These substances decompose rapidly in the environment. This characteristic is not true of the second group—the chlorinated hydrocarbons—of which DDT is the most famous example.

DDT was first made in 1874 by a German research chemist who was investigating the interaction of sulfuric acid with various carbon compounds in the laboratory of Dr. Emil Fischer of Strassburg. DDT's chemical formula is $C_{14}H_9Cl_5$, and its chemical name is dichloro-diphenyl-trichloroethane.

DDT's effectiveness as an insecticide was first realized in 1939, some sixty-five years after it was initially described, by a Swiss chemist, Dr. Paul Mueller. In 1948, less than ten years later, Sweden awarded Mueller the Nobel Prize for Chemistry because of his discovery of DDT's "miraculous" capacity for destroying insects. After another twenty years, during which some of DDT's less desirable effects had been documented, Sweden was the first country in the world to ban entirely the use of DDT within its borders.

The Use of DDT

DDT's effectiveness as a deadly insect killer was discovered just in time for it to be of extensive service during the Second World War. The U. S. Army used it in February, 1944, to halt a typhus epidemic in Naples, Italy, dusting it in powder form on inhabitants to destroy body lice, the carriers of the disease. DDT was also used very effectively all over the world to combat flies and mosquitoes—especially the dreaded *Anopheles* mosquito, the carrier of malaria.

Once the Second World War was over, DDT was released for domestic use in the United States in 1946. The U. S. Department of Agriculture hailed it as a

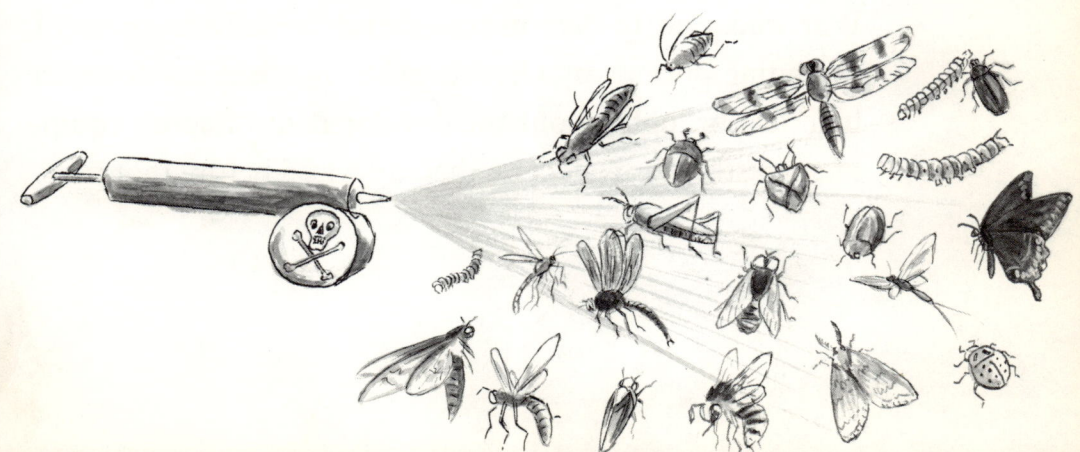

chemical cure-all, which would eliminate all sorts of agricultural pests. The Forest Service of the Department of Agriculture thought it would be especially useful for conquering the gypsy moth and wiping out its potential threat to forests. As a first step toward that goal, a twenty-acre woodlot near Wilkes-Barre, heavily infested with gypsy moths, was sprayed with DDT by airplane in the spring of 1946. Such complete eradication of the moth occurred that not a single larva could be found in spite of the fact that cash prizes were offered to anyone who did. In 1948, just two years later, 1250 square miles of the State of Pennsylvania were sprayed from the air with DDT to wipe out other infestations of the species.

The Air Age in Insect Control

The rapid pace of research during the Second World War had clearly demonstrated the full effectiveness of spreading poisons by air. Advances in chemical research had also brought about the development of spray equipment vastly more effective than any used before that time.

Because of such advances, a new air age in insect control quickly developed after the war. By 1952, more than 5000 airplanes in the United States were equipped for spraying insecticides, and this armada of pest-control aircraft was logging nearly 500,000 hours each year.

Many of these aircraft were small two-seater biplanes, with 90- to 110-gallon tanks for insecticides located in the forward cockpit. These little planes usually flew about 50 feet above the ground or treetops and sprayed a strip approximately 100 feet wide beneath them. But planes as large as the twin-engined C-47, the workhorse transport and cargo plane of the Second World War, were also used. Converted for spraying, the C-47 carried two tanks with a combined capacity of almost 1000 gallons of poison. Flying 150 to 200 feet above the trees, the C-47 could blanket an area about 600 feet wide with insecticide. "One C-47 cargo plane," an expert declared, "could with one load of insecticide treat as large an area as could be covered by one truck-borne spray rig in four years—and more effectively."

Trapping Male Moths

By 1949, continuing research by the Department of Agriculture indicated that DDT, dissolved in fuel oil and sprayed at a rate of one pound of the insecticide per acre, would kill all the caterpillars in that area. Later the staff determined that a half pound per acre was almost as effective. In view of the success of the 1948 aerial spraying in Pennsylvania, the Department of Agriculture decided that the time was ripe for launching a general attack on the gypsy moth, using DDT. The first step in the campaign would be the reestablishment of a successful barrier zone to prevent the moth's spread. Once again the ultimate goal was the extermination of the moth in North America.

As a preliminary tactic, some 20,000 traps were set out in New York, Pennsylvania, New Jersey, Connecticut, and Rhode Island to check for the moth's presence. The trap used was merely a sealed paper cup with a small entrance hole at one end. The inside was coated with a sticky substance. Male moths could enter

the cup, but they could seldom escape. The trap was baited with "essence of female gypsy moth," which was made at that time by capturing female moths and snipping off the last segment of their abdomen, which contained the scent glands. This natural sex lure was then distilled in benzene and used to bait the traps.

Such traps, distributed throughout forest areas, were sure to attract nearby male moths, thus demonstrating their presence in the area. The region could then be slated for spraying. In 1950, as a result of such trapping efforts, more than 600,000 acres in the Northeast were sprayed with DDT.

That year and the next, populations of gypsy moths seemed to be at a low ebb all over the insect's range. During the next several years, however, its numbers were on the rise nearly everywhere. By 1956, the species had invaded some nine million previously uninfected acres in New York and Pennsylvania, and it had reappeared in New Jersey. In addition, an isolated colony was found in far-off Michigan. How it had become established there, no one knew.

Intensive Spraying of 1957

Administrators of the Plant Pest Control Branch of the Department of Agriculture were those most immediately concerned about the moth's spread. In their judgment, a more intensive program of DDT spraying needed to be undertaken at once. In this way, they said, the moth could possibly be eradicated completely. The cost of such a campaign would be between thirty and thirty-five million dollars.

Detailed plans were drawn up, with the immediate goals of exterminating the gypsy moth in Michigan, Pennsylvania, and New Jersey. Also, it was to be cleared out of the protective barrier zone in New York State.

Almost a million acres had been sprayed with DDT in the 1956 gypsy-moth campaign. Plans for 1957 were even more extensive, for Congress had voted additional funds for the project. More than 36,000 gypsy-moth traps were set in an arc 75 to 100 miles wide, from Red Bank, New Jersey, to eastern Maine, to check areas of infestation. As a result, the 1957 program called for spraying three million acres of the Northeast—the largest single campaign of spraying ever done in the United States. Counting state and local spraying as well, more than five million acres of infested woodland were finally treated with DDT that year.

As one small part of this grandiose operation, Nassau County on Long Island was scheduled for spraying in the spring of 1957. Learning of the plans, a number of concerned citizens—among them Dr. Robert Cushman Murphy, a world-renowned ornithologist—started legal action to block the proposed spraying. By the time the petition was heard in court, the spraying had already occurred, however, and the judge ruled against the petition as "after the fact."

The gypsy-moth population of Nassau County was fairly low that spring, but the widespread use of DDT caused unpleasant side effects. Many people were showered from the air with the spray made up of DDT dissolved in fuel oil. Raining down, the poison splattered indiscriminately on gypsy-moth caterpillars, other insects, birds, cats, dogs, cows, horses, children, laundry, and other vulnerable animals and objects. Most of the people who were victims of the spraying were quite unhappy about it.

Undaunted by their initial legal defeat, Murphy and his group of aroused environmentalists continued their court battle, trying to block any future spraying of their properties. The resultant widely publicized confrontation —with many expert witnesses called by both sides—was called the Gypsy Moth Trial, or the DDT Trial. It finally ended with a State Supreme Court judge ruling against the complainants, stating that no proven harm or hardship had been demonstrated as a result of the previous spraying.

Although they were the legal losers in the Gypsy Moth Trial, the aroused citizens were really the victors, for they achieved what they had been working for: limitations on indiscriminate aerial spraying of DDT. The court battle had received wide publicity and had alerted the public to some of DDT's dangerous side effects. Also, scientists were learning more about these undesirable effects all the time.

Harmful Effects of DDT

DDT and its chlorinated hydrocarbon relatives—aldrin, dieldrin, endrin, chlordane, heptachlor, and lindane—are all long-lived persistent poisons that remain in the soil in lethal strength for many years. All seven dissolve only very slightly in water, but they can be dissolved and stored very readily in fatty tissues of living things. Washing into streams, the poison is picked up by the smallest animals in the food chain and then passed on to larger

animals that eat them. Step by step the DDT becomes concentrated in ever more deadly doses.

Evidence of the resulting damage was turning up everywhere. The death of thousands of robins in East Lansing, Michigan, was traced to the spraying of elm trees with DDT for Dutch elm disease in the spring of 1955 and succeeding years. Spectacular fish kills were being recorded all over the country as a result of spraying campaigns with DDT or related pesticides.

Even more alarming were investigations into the failure to reproduce, and the slow disappearance, of fish- and flesh-eating birds such as eagles, falcons, ospreys, and pelicans. DDT was the suspected cause of this reproductive failure, but years of research were needed to prove the point. Absorbed along with the fish or small mammals that such birds eat, DDT accumulates in the birds' bodies and acts to prevent the manufacture of calcium carbonate, the vital ingredient of eggshell. As a consequence, the birds frequently do not lay any eggs at all, or they lay eggs with shells so thin that they break long before they can hatch. In other cases, the young birds die before hatching or shortly thereafter.

Soon after the Long Island spraying against the gypsy moth, traces of DDT began to show up in cows' milk. Under existing health standards, such milk was unsaleable. Farmers, absorbing huge dairy losses, were outraged. More frightening yet, DDT was also being discovered in human milk, in some cases at greater concentrations than in cows' milk. A number of respected scientists were now voicing deep concern about DDT's possible future effects upon human beings as well as other forms of life.

With the public outcry becoming ever more vocal, the Department of Agriculture quickly reduced its use of DDT. In 1958, the Government sprayed only half a million acres against the gypsy moth, compared to three million or more acres the year before. In 1959, the figures dropped to just 100,000 acres. And on Long Island, despite the widespread spraying of 1957, gypsy moths reappeared in considerable numbers.

DDT and its related chlorinated hydrocarbons fell into even more disrepute in 1962 when the book *Silent Spring* by Rachel Carson was published. This famous work graphically portrayed many of the ill effects caused by indiscriminate use of insecticides. Top officials of both the Department of Agriculture and the chemical industry promptly derided the book as inaccurate and alarmist, but many responsible scientists just as quickly rose to its defense. The next year President Kennedy's Science Advisory Committee also warned that: "Elimination of the use of persistent toxic pesticides should be the goal."

DDT Dies Hard

Since that time, the use of such poisons has decreased year by year in the United States, as less persistent pesticides and other types of control have been developed. In 1969, Michigan outlawed the sale of DDT, the first state to do so. By 1971, the United States allowed DDT to be sprayed only in emergencies in which no effective alternate was available. The era of mass spraying with DDT in the United States seemed to be over. But because of global circulation patterns, this long-lived poison continues to contaminate fish throughout the seas and animals throughout the world—from Arctic reindeer to Antarctic penguins.

Many working in pest control, many officials of the Department of Agriculture, and many in the chemical industry have never been convinced, however, that DDT is other than a great blessing to all mankind. Through the years they have continued to urge its use as one of the most effective insecticides ever made.

As recently as the fall of 1973, when the tussock moth was enjoying a population explosion in the forests of the far West, proponents of mass spraying immediately urged the use of DDT to suppress the pest. The Environmental Protection Agency, which had been created by the president in the fall of 1970 to regulate actions affecting the environment, at first stood firm against the proposal. Chemical lobbyists, however, managed to get bills allowing DDT to be used in the tussock moth "emergency" introduced in Congress. In the spring of 1974 the agency reluctantly authorized its emergency use.

DDT has a long life, as we have seen, and the question of its use in the United States—and in many other countries throughout the world—is still very much alive today.

Other Chemicals Used

The gypsy moth quickly recovered from the mass sprayings with DDT of the 1950's, and its range spread as never before. Other insecticides, accordingly, began to be used in place of DDT. Foremost among them was a less persistent compound called carbaryl—usually known by the trade name of Sevin. This insecticide came

into wide use in the 1960's as the use of DDT declined and was the first one licensed by the Environmental Protection Agency for aerial spraying of gypsy moths.

Sevin is largely broken down chemically within a few days or weeks, as compared to many years for DDT, and does not accumulate in body tissues. Quite effective against most caterpillars, it has the disadvantage of affecting other organisms as well and is particularly deadly to bees. Because it breaks down quickly, several sprayings per season are often needed. Laboratory research also indicates that carbaryl may cause birth defects in mice, chicks, and other small vertebrate animals.

Besides Sevin, several organic phosphate compounds are presently being used to kill the gypsy moth, and still other compounds are constantly being tested. Every year chemical companies develop new insecticides that they hope to be able to market and sell. Samples of these experimental compounds are sent to the Department of Agriculture for testing at one of their laboratories.

One of these laboratories is the Gypsy Moth Methods Improvement Laboratory on the grounds of Otis Air Force Base on Cape Cod. There scientists carry on extensive tests of new insecticides and also raise gypsy-moth caterpillars in mass numbers for insecticide testing and other research purposes.

When samples of new insecticides are received at the laboratory, the staff painstakingly tests each of them in various solutions and strengths. Then their effects on laboratory-raised gypsy caterpillars are recorded. The test insecticide is also sprayed in carefully calculated dosages on seedling oak trees in the laboratory, and newly hatched caterpillars are placed on the trees. The staff observes both the fate of the caterpillars and the degree of defoliation of the trees over a period of days.

Testing New Insecticides in the Field

When a particular chemical shows promise in the laboratory, it is tried out under natural conditions in a wooded area where there is a current outbreak of gypsy moths. Three test areas of fifty acres each are usually mapped out in such an infested region, and the corners of these areas are marked by large white bags tied to the very tops of trees. In this way the boundaries of the test areas can be spotted easily from an airplane. At the proper time, a small plane sprays each test area with the trial insecticide, but it leaves areas between them unsprayed for later comparison.

Spraying must be timed properly to gauge the effectiveness of an insecticide. Most compounds used against the gypsy moth are spread soon after the caterpillars hatch, when the trees are just beginning to leaf out. A hard rain may wash the poison from the foliage and make another spraying necessary. A brisk wind will carry the insecticide into areas not slated for spraying.

To figure the effects of test sprayings, five small study areas, each a tenth of an acre, are marked out at random in each fifty-acre test plot. In each of these small study areas, counts of gypsy egg masses are made before spraying. After the spraying, white drop cloths are placed on the ground at various spots in the test patches, and daily counts are made of the dead larvae collected on the drop cloths. Later in the season the areas are checked to record the amount of foliage eaten by caterpillars, and the condition of surviving larvae and pupae is studied. During the fall another egg count is made for comparison purposes.

If detailed and extensive tests show promising results for a particular chemical, it is subjected to other experiments designed to show its effect on laboratory animals and upon the environment. Sometimes a compound may undergo years of testing before it is either turned down or given a stamp of approval by the Environmental Protection Agency and registered for use against particular insects.

Most states have pesticide boards that also rule on the use of each pesticide within that state. In addition, they test and license the individuals who will do the actual spraying. Long experience has shown that all of these procedures and safeguards are needed before an insecticide is licensed for general use.

V
Biological Controls

In her book, *Silent Spring,* Rachel Carson noted that "The really effective control of insects is that applied by nature, not man. Populations are kept in check by something the ecologists call the resistance of the environment, and this has been so since the first life was created."

In recent years more and more agricultural scientists have agreed with that statement as the hazards and failures of chemical warfare against insects have become increasingly evident. As a result, research into the possibilities of using natural biological controls against pests has been intensified.

The population of every insect—indeed, every living thing—is influenced and kept in check by various natural controls. Once the population of an elephant, a mouse, or an insect becomes too numerous in any given area, these natural checks and balances take effect. Enemies increase, starvation and disease take their toll, and the population inevitably falls. In time, conditions become favorable to the species once more, and the population starts an upswing. Such ups and downs, which happen to gypsy moths as well as to every other species, are known as the balance of nature.

Natural Balance

Local populations of gypsy moths, observers note, rise and fall in irregular cycles. For years there may be very few gypsy moths in a forested area. Under favorable conditions, however, the population may gradually build up. One summer it finally reaches a peak—sometimes there are millions of caterpillars per acre—and whole forests may be stripped of their leaves. But diseases and natural enemies eventually cause the population to fall, and for years afterward the moth's numbers may be so reduced in the area that it poses no problem.

Scientists point out that natural controls tend to be permanent; many of them are living organisms that can reproduce as long as weather and food supplies remain favorable. Insecticides, on the other hand, assure only the temporary destruction of a pest in a given area.

Chemical controls, they also note, often upset the natural balance by killing natural enemies of the pest as well as the pest.

By using and manipulating natural biological controls, scientists hope that they can keep the populations of gypsy moths and other pests to tolerable levels. Regulatory in nature, such biological controls are in the long run safer and more economical to use than insecticides.

Those who fought the gypsy moth in the 1890's noted that various birds were enemies of the insect. Flycatchers pursue and eat the flying moths. Woodpeckers and nuthatches eat the pupae, and thrushes, grackles, blue jays, orioles, and many other species prey on the caterpillars. The black-billed and yellow-billed cuckoos are probably the champion gypsy-caterpillar destroyers of all the birds. Cuckoos are not common birds in New England, but they are so fond of the hairy larvae that whenever there is an outbreak of gypsy moths, the cuckoo population of that region often increases too.

Birds, however, are not the only vertebrate enemies of the gypsy moth. Many small mammals also prey on it. Skunks eat the pupae, and shrews and moles undoubtedly take their share. Mice, especially the white-footed mouse, are particularly important predators. These engaging little rodents relish the pupae and are often abundant in woodlands where outbreaks of the gypsy moth occur. Field biologists are so optimistic about the possibility of the white-footed mouse helping to curb gypsy-moth populations that they are stepping up their studies of mouse activities, population dynamics, and mortality factors.

Insect Parasites and Predators

The most work, however, has been done with insect enemies of the gypsy moth. As Dr. Howard noted in 1906, the gypsy moth has many such natural enemies in Europe and Asia, and they reduce gypsy-moth numbers effectively. Many of these insect enemies have been naturalized in the United States and have proved helpful in controlling the moth here.

The program of raising and releasing these insect enemies continues today. From 1963 until 1970, for example, New Jersey raised and released some eighty million gypsy-moth parasites, forty million of them in 1970 alone. At least eight species of these Old World parasites are now well established in the northeastern United States. Most of them are native to Europe, but one comes from Japan, and several originated in India. They include an ichneumon wasp, a braconid wasp, and several tiny chalcid wasps and tachinid flies. Some attack the caterpillars, others the pupae, and still others the eggs of gypsy moths. Most of them lay their eggs in or on the host. After hatching, the parasitic larva feeds on the tissues of its host until it completes development. Then it emerges and spins its cocoon, and the gypsy host dies.

One of the most effective parasites is a tiny chalcid wasp from Japan (*Ooencyrtus kuwanae*), which has several generations each year and lays its eggs upon gypsy-moth eggs. This parasite may infest sixty to ninety percent of the eggs during a gypsy-moth outbreak.

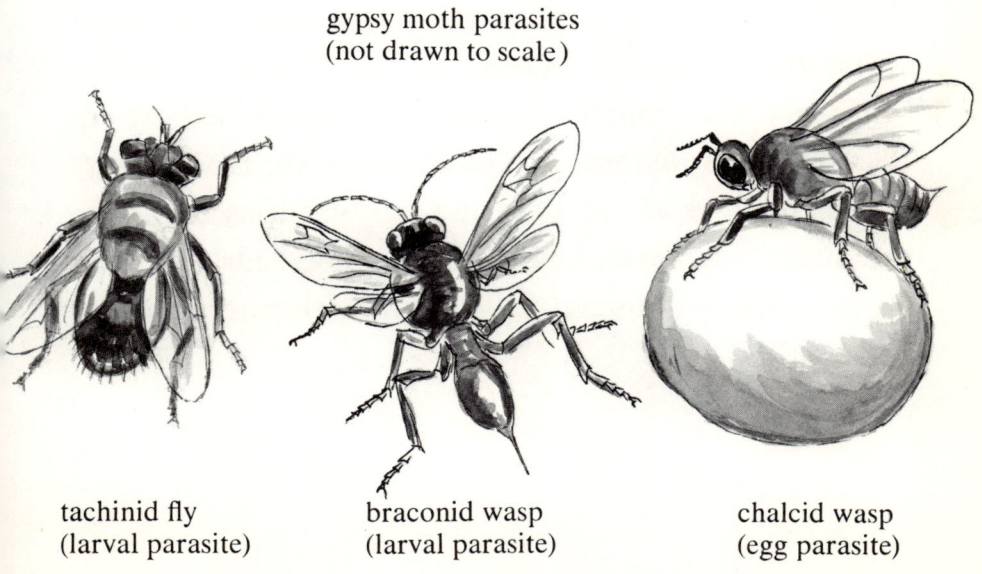

gypsy moth parasites
(not drawn to scale)

tachinid fly
(larval parasite)

braconid wasp
(larval parasite)

chalcid wasp
(egg parasite)

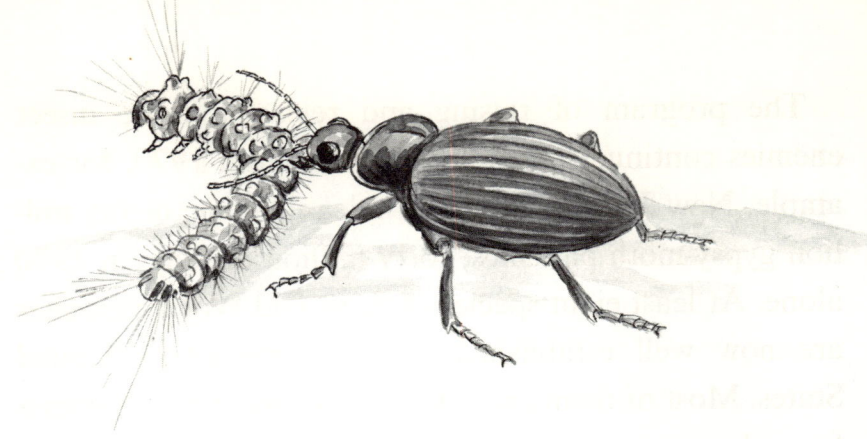

Another, a tachinid fly, lays its eggs on foliage, and the parasite gains entrance into the gypsy caterpillar when the caterpillar eats the leaf bearing the fly's egg.

Several predatory beetles are also effective enemies of the gypsy moth. One, a large ground beetle (*Calosoma sycophanta*) native to Europe, has been naturalized in the United States. Both the adult beetle and its larva feed voraciously upon gypsy caterpillars. Aptly called caterpillar hunters, the adult beetles sometimes live four years or more, and a pair of them may eat nearly 300 large caterpillars in one season. A native American beetle, which is a close relative of the European species, also hunts caterpillars and may help to control the gypsy moth.

Viral and Bacterial Infections

Like other animals, insects are often killed by infectious virus diseases. Fortunately for us, these insect-killing diseases are very specific and, so far as is known, are harmless to man. One of them, a polyhedral-forming virus called wilt disease, kills gypsy-moth caterpillars by attacking the caterpillar's blood cells and causing them to disintegrate. The victim loses its appetite and becomes sluggish and inactive. Finally it dies, its body hanging from a branch like a sack full of putrefying liquid.

The liquid contains billions of microscopic polyhedral virus bodies that enclose the living virus. The polyhedral bodies are pure white and heavier than water. They are presently being isolated from infected larvae in research laboratories by grinding up the caterpillars in a watery suspension. The resultant mixture is filtered through cheesecloth, and much of the debris—caterpillar heads, skin, and bristles—are then removed by centrifugal force. The refined pellets of polyhedral virus that remain are air-dried and stored under refrigeration.

Scientists believe that these processed pellets of polyhedral virus can be introduced into local outbreaks of gypsy-moth caterpillars and used to help control them. Quickly spreading from one caterpillar to another, the virus often causes massive mortality.

The polyhedral bodies of a similar virus of the European spruce sawfly have already been used very effectively in the same way that chemical sprays are used. Virus diseases of other insects are being tested today, and some experts believe that the gypsy moth's virus disease may eventually become the principal control of the pest.

Bacteria also can help to control insect pests. One of the first used for this purpose was the bacterium that causes milky disease in Japanese beetle grubs.

Another bacterial disease, *Bacillus thuringiensis* (Bt), infects caterpillars of the gypsy moth and other species. Like the milky disease of Japanese beetle grubs, Bt undergoes an active, multiplying period called the vegetative cell stage. At this time it flourishes in a moist environment, such as the gut of a gypsy-moth caterpillar. As the Bt vegetative cells increase, they produce poisonous by-products that kill the caterpillar. But as nourishment for these vegetative cells becomes exhausted, they cease to multiply, and a hardy, heat-resistant spore is formed. The spore is inactive and can survive long periods of unfavorable environment. When suitable conditions return, active vegetative cells begin to be produced once again.

Commercial preparations of *Bacillus thuringiensis*, made up of the spores and their by-products, are presently being produced. These preparations can be sprayed on foliage. Gypsy-moth caterpillars eat the leaves, become infected, and die after their digestive tracts stop functioning. One commercial preparation of Bt is called Thuricide, another Dipel. Both can be fairly effective in preventing defoliation in areas infested with gypsy moths. Wherever they are sprayed, however, they kill the larvae of all kinds of moths and butterflies that are present.

Scent Traps

Entomologists have long studied the ability of female moths to release a scent that attracts male moths to them. One of the first to conduct experiments on this power was the famous French naturalist, Jean Henri Fabre,

who worked with the great peacock moth of Europe, about 100 years ago.

In recent years, entomologists have done a great deal of research on the scent released by female gypsy moths. As early as the 1890's, experiments were conducted in which female gypsy moths were placed in traps and observed while male moths flew to them. During the 1950's, the natural lure was extracted and used extensively in traps to check the presence of moths in particular areas.

Eventually a method of manufacturing the scent synthetically in the laboratory was devised, after chemists had analyzed the natural product and determined its molecular structure. This synthetic lure, called Disparlure, was first created in 1970 by Dr. Morton Beroza of the Entomology Research Division of the United States Department of Agriculture. The manufactured lure attracts male moths even more strongly than the natural scent and is now widely used as bait in traps for catching male moths.

Theoretically if all the male moths in any area are trapped, the females will be unable to mate and lay fertile eggs. Such a result, however, has never been achieved, even though many thousands of cardboard traps have been scattered over infested areas by plane in hopes of such results.

Recently the Department of Agriculture has experimented with a "confusion" technique, the blanketing of an entire area with Disparlure in the hope of confusing the male moths so that they cannot find mates. Bits of paper or cork are soaked with the synthetic scent, and then hundreds of thousands of these particles are showered down upon an area from an airplane. Sometimes the scent is enclosed in tiny gelatin capsules, which stick to foliage. With the female scent everywhere in equal strength throughout an area, the male moths presumably are unable to locate females. Results achieved with this method so far are uncertain. The technique might work where there are very few moths, but if gypsy moths are abundant, a certain number of males are almost sure to find mates in spite of distracting scents.

Insect Sterilization

Many years ago a far-seeing scientist, Dr. Edward E. Knipling, Director of the Entomology Research Division of the Department of Agriculture, pondered the possibilities of controlling or eradicating insect pests by sterilizing one sex or the other by radiation or chemical treatment. In this way the female might be caused to lay infertile eggs after mating.

After years of effort, Knipling and his colleagues eventually demonstrated the practicality of such a method in the case of the screwworm fly, a pest that afflicted cattle in Southern states. Raising screwworm flies by the billions in huge breeding factories, Knipling and his staff sterilized specimens of both sexes by subjecting them to radioactive cobalt treatments. The sterilized insects were then released in infected areas. The sterilized males mated with wild females, which mate only once. As a result, the females laid infertile eggs, and the overall population was reduced in the next generation. Repeating this process with many generations, the screwworm fly was exterminated completely, first on the island of Curaçao and then in Florida. Excellent results have also been achieved in Texas and other Southwestern states, but reinfestation by screwworm flies from Mexico remains a problem.

screwworm fly

Using the same technique, fruit flies have been eliminated on certain Pacific islands. Because of these successes, Knipling became known as "the father of insect birth control."

A technique for sterilizing the male pupae of gypsy moths in the laboratory by gamma radiation has now been developed, and further research into the possibilities of controlling gypsy moths in the wild by the release of sterile individuals is now under way. There are a number of hurdles to be overcome, however, before this technique can be perfected. Chief among them is the fact that gypsy moths have a much longer life cycle then screw-worm flies and are much harder and more expensive to raise in quantity in the laboratory.

As well as sterilizing insects by radiation, scientists are also investigating various methods of sterilizing them with chemicals. Certain chemicals retard the growth of insect reproductive organs. Sprayed on trees, or fed to the insects, such chemicals could render the insects incapable of breeding.

Some investigators voice the hope of developing, through selective breeding, a "strong race" of gypsy moths in the future, a race that would carry a high incidence of crippling or harmful genes that they would pass on to their offspring. As the lethal genes are spread throughout the population, the species would be crippled.

One possibility turned up by this research is the introduction into the United States of the Japanese race of the gypsy moth. Preliminary experiments indicate that when a male Japanese gypsy moth mates with a female American moth, the resultant cross carries the seeds of its own destruction. The female hybrids are sterile and intersexual (intermediate in sexual characteristics between a typical male and female). The hybrid males are fertile, but when they mate with American females, half of the resultant females are also sterile and intersexual.

The Juvenile Hormone

In order to grow and develop, every insect must molt its skin from time to time. The molting process is set in motion by a secretion from special neurosecretory cells in the insect's brain.

This brain hormone acts on glands in the insect's head and thorax, and these glands in turn secrete the molting hormone that enables the insect to shed its skin. If some way could be found to inhibit the secretion of this molting hormone, the insect would fail to molt its skin and would die. Dr. Maria Bade, a Boston College scientist, is presently investigating the possibilities of this approach, using the tobacco hornworm—the caterpillar of a sphinx moth —as her laboratory subject.

A great deal of research has already been done on another aspect of insect growth and development: the

tobacco hornworm and shed skin

role played by a mysterious and powerful substance known as the juvenile hormone. This hormone is secreted by two tiny bodies called the *corpora allata* in the insect's brain. As long as the juvenile hormone is present when an immature insect molts, the insect remains a larva after the molt. The gypsy caterpillar, for example, sheds its skin five or six times as it grows from a tiny larva less than a quarter of an inch long to a bristly two-inch-long caterpillar.

Once the caterpillar reaches its full growth, its *corpora allata* cease production of the juvenile hormone. At the next molt the caterpillar transforms to a pupa, at the next to an adult moth.

If the glands producing the juvenile hormone are transplanted experimentally from an immature caterpillar to a maturing one, the maturing caterpillar does not pupate

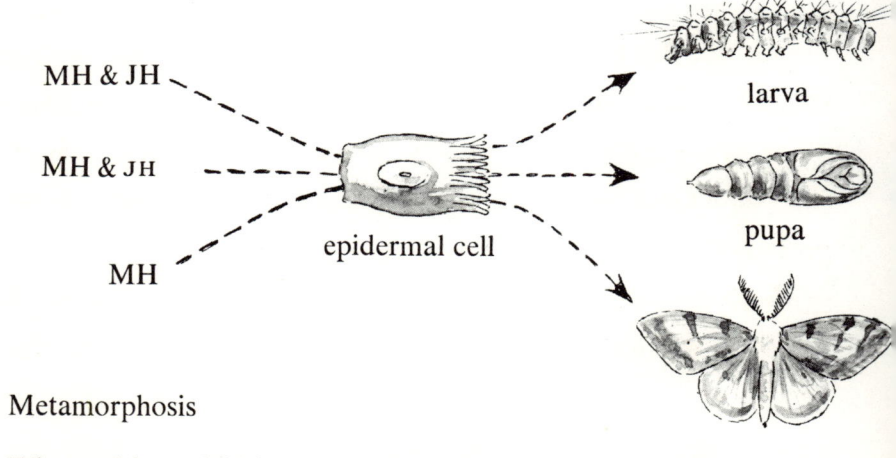

Metamorphosis

When epidermal (skin) cells are acted upon by molting hormone (MH) together with juvenile hormone (JH), insect remains a larva after the molt. When only a small amount of juvenile hormone (JH) is present, larva becomes a pupa. If only MH is present, an adult insect develops.

(*after Wigglesworth*)

and continues to grow as a larva. On the other hand, if the glands are removed from an immature or half-grown caterpillar, its supply of the juvenile hormone is cut off prematurely. Then it quickly pupates and transforms into a miniature adult.

This juvenile hormone was first studied in detail by Dr. Carroll Williams of Harvard, who worked with Cecropia moths. He isolated the hormone in 1956 and worked out its chemical structure. As a result, a synthetic substitute for the juvenile hormone was eventually created in the laboratory.

By spraying caterpillars with a synthesis of their juvenile hormone, it may eventually be possible to prevent them from metamorphizing and becoming adults. The immature larvae might then become harmless monsters, unable either to eat or reproduce.

Rivers of Natural Insecticides

In 1964, Dr. Williams and a colleague, Dr. Karel Sláma, investigated a related hormonal phenomenon. They were baffled by the fact that linden bugs, which they were raising in the laboratory, never became adults and remained juveniles until they died. The bugs did go through several extra larval molts, however, and became juvenile giants, larger than normal but unable to reproduce.

Through a series of experiments the two scientists discovered that a specific substance was preventing the development of the linden bugs. It proved to be a chemical factor, or hormone, which was present in strips of paper toweling in the insect containers. The paper was made from the wood of balsam fir trees. Ages ago, they theorized, the balsam fir began to produce this hormone as a natural defense against insect pests that attacked them. Now it was activating the juvenile hormone of linden bugs and preventing them from maturing.

The scientists called this mysterious substance the paper factor since they first noted its effect in paper used in the linden-bug containers. Further research shows that certain other trees manufacture similar chemicals, which act in the same way to inhibit the development of various groups of insects. Today synthetic insect juvenile hormones have been prepared from such plant substances.

Dr. Williams and his colleagues have also discovered the substance in various bodies of water after vegetable matter has been steeped in the water and the substance released. One such place is the Rio Negro of Brazil. Winding its way through dense jungles, this river collects the paper factor from decaying vegetation. Thus, the Rio Negro, as one entomologist remarked after noting the scarcity of insects in the region, is a "river of natural insecticides."

Eventually these natural insecticides may be used against many kinds of insect pests. A great deal of further research will be necessary, however, and precautions will need to be taken to ensure that beneficial insects or other forms of life are not affected by the application of such substances.

Insect Repellents

Scientists are also studying the effects of various repellents and stimulants on insects. An insect repellent is a substance or condition that keeps insects away from certain objects or areas. Smoke and citronella, for example, are mosquito repellents. Entomologists theorize that they might be able to develop some chemical which would keep gypsy or other caterpillars from attacking certain trees.

The leaves of ash, tulip poplar, and several other trees are almost always refused by gypsy caterpillars, even though they eat hundreds of other kinds of leaves. Do these leaves contain some natural substance—some paper factor— that repels the gypsy caterpillar?

A Princeton University biologist, Dr. Vincent Dethier, is presently studying the tastes of caterpillars. Attaching electrodes to the taste and smell centers of their nervous systems, he records the caterpillars' responses as various food solutions are presented to them. By "wiretapping the caterpillar's nervous system," he hopes eventually to be able to isolate the substances that either repel or attract various larvae. A discovery of this sort might prove very valuable in the future for protecting forest and shade trees from ravages by gypsy and other caterpillars.

An entirely different type of insect repellent is a sound barrier that could be set up to prevent various insects from entering certain areas, such as orchards. Many moths have "ears" located on the thorax. These organs are very sensitive to certain high-frequency sounds, such as the ultrasonic squeaks that bats send out as they hunt for food. Spreading out ahead of the bat, the sound waves bounce back from solid objects such as trees, warning the bat to swerve and avoid the object. But when the sound waves hit a small moving object, such as a moth, they signal "food" to the bat, and it swoops to catch the insect. On the other hand, the moth "hears" the bat squeaks, too, and drops suddenly or takes evasive action to avoid capture.

Canadian research has demonstrated that an ultrasonic "fence" set up around an orchard may effectively bar certain pest moths from entering the orchard.

Raising Caterpillars for Research

Many of the gypsy caterpillars used in laboratory research are raised in a large breeding house at the Gypsy Moth Methods Improvement Laboratory on Cape Cod. Eggs are gathered during the summer and, after the embryonic young have developed, are stored for several months or more in refrigerators at temperatures ranging from thirty-four to forty degrees. When brought out of this artificial winter into warm-room temperatures, the eggs hatch after a few days.

The larvae are fed a laboratory-created food made by mixing wheat germ, vitamins, oils, and minerals necessary to the diet with an agar, or gelatin, base. Artificial flavoring and coloring are sometimes added. After being mixed and cooked, the caterpillar food is poured into pans. When it has cooled and stiffened, it is cut into half-inch squares. These food units are stored and fed to the newly hatched larvae as needed. Larger caterpillars are given the same mixture poured into small paper cups.

Using methods such as these, many thousands of gypsy caterpillars are raised for experimentation throughout most of the year. The embryonic larva must undergo a period of low temperatures before it hatches from the egg, however. This factor makes it difficult to raise sufficient numbers of gypsy moths in the laboratory for sterilization and other research programs.

In order for a sterilization program to be successful, many millions of laboratory-raised gypsy moths would be required. One scientist estimates that at least 50 to 100 sterilized moths would be needed for every wild and fertile specimen.

With current methods of raising gypsy moths, such a ratio would be impossible to achieve. In hopes of speeding up the moth's life-cycle, however, Department of Agriculture entomologists placed 1000 gypsy-moth eggs in Skylab—the United States space station—in the fall of 1973. This experiment is intended to check the effect of zero gravity on the time of hatching. Earlier Skylab experiments showed that lack of gravity may produce cell changes in plants. The officials theorize that zero gravity might liberate larval hormones causing the gypsy-moth caterpillars to hatch early. If so, the discovery could lead to more successful methods of raising large numbers of moths under artificial conditions. Few scientists, however, voice much hope for this line of research.

VI
Prescription Entomology

A great deal of the basic research on biological controls of insects is carried on at the Department of Agriculture's Research Service Center in Beltsville, Maryland. There, on a site covering more than 10,000 acres, are located some seventy laboratories, forty greenhouses, and hundreds of barns and other buildings. The research program at Beltsville continually works to discover new ways of improving agricultural crops and insect-pest controls.

This research, however, is just one small part of the Department of Agriculture. The vast government agency regulates and oversees our production of food crops, and it also administers our forest lands and our soil conservation programs. The Department supports basic research at many colleges and universities and administers many regional insect-pest laboratories, such as the gypsy-moth facilities on Cape Cod.

Four different departments or agencies of the Department of Agriculture are directly concerned with the control of gypsy moths. They are:

1. The Animal and Plant Health Inspection Service, called APHIS for short. This agency conducts surveys of gypsy-moth populations and enforces the quarantine to prevent spreading.

2. The Agricultural Research Service (ARS), which conducts basic research on various methods of fighting the pest.

3. The Extension Service, which functions as an informational agency. It produces and distributes leaflets and other educational material about the gypsy moth.

4. The Forest Service, which conducts research on the gypsy moth in forest areas and coordinates Federal and state control programs.

Each state, of course, has the equivalent of these Federal agricultural services. In addition, a National Gypsy Moth Advisory Council has been formed to lobby for research funds and to correlate and publicize all of the current information about the moth gathered by Federal and state investigators. The Council is made up of a number of official government representatives, a number representing industries dealing in forest products, and members of various citizen groups.

Integrated Pest Control

Before 1945, programs for controlling insect pests were conducted for the most part on a piecemeal basis. Insecticides, biological-control methods, and pest-resistant crops were developed and studied independently.

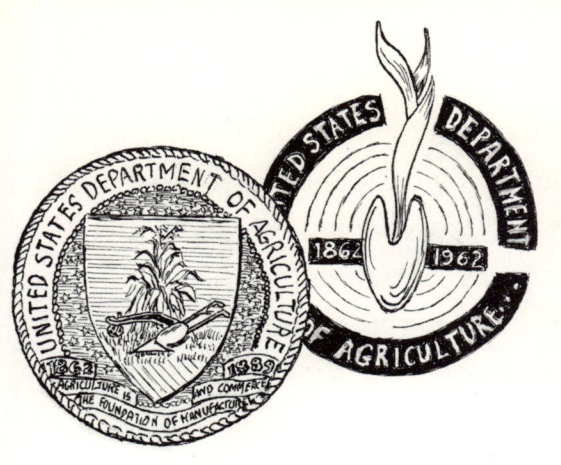

Very few people considered the possibilities of coordinating all of these approaches into integrated programs designed to solve the problems of a particular crop, pest, or situation.

Today, however, many scientists promote the idea of integrated pest control, the use of any and every method that would prove helpful in a particular situation. Some people call this approach prescription entomology, an ecologically slanted control plan to fit each situation.

Integrated control does not aim to exterminate an insect pest. Rather it aims to control it and keep its populations within reasonable limits, so that it does not do any extensive damage.

"Hard" pesticides, the persistent chlorinated hydrocarbons, have very doubtful value in any system of integrated control. "DDT is incompatible with integrated control," one research entomologist has said, "because it disrupts the beneficial balance of insect communities, often creates greater pest problems than it solves, is destructive to wildlife, and is a human health hazard."

For gypsy moths, integrated control means that parasites and other suitable biological controls will be used when practical, but that insecticides will be applied only in particular restricted areas. Street shade trees, for example, might be sprayed from the ground with an approved nonpersistent insecticide such as Sevin, but not an entire town or region from the air.

Enforcing the Quarantine

Along with integrated control, the quarantine on gypsy moths is being continued in an effort to prevent or slow the insect's spread. The moth has turned up in a number of new states during the past several years—Virginia, West Virginia, North and South Carolina, Florida, Tennessee, and Iowa among others. Foresters are alarmed at this rapid widening of the gypsy moth's range. If the species should invade Southern forests in strength, they fear that it would inflict many millions of dollars' worth of damage to timber in the Appalachians.

As a result, the Department of Agriculture has intensified its Stop-the-Gypsy-Moth campaign. Not all roads or vehicles can be checked in our traveling society, however, and inspections are concentrated in state or Federal campgrounds where the touring public parks its campers and trailers for several days or weeks at a time.

Federal employees inspect vehicles before they leave, checking to see whether they harbor any gypsy-moth caterpillars, pupae, or egg clusters. Doing a thorough job is almost impossible, however, and in spite of every effort the gypsy moth continues to spread.

Opposing Points of View

During the past 100 years Americans have probably spent over a hundred million dollars—some say much more—in the continuing effort to exterminate or control the gypsy moth. Today various organizations urge even greater efforts against it than ever before. Among them are the Department of Agriculture, various forestry and

lumbering groups, spokesmen for the pesticide industry, and many who make their living by dealing with tourists in recreational areas. They say that the moth has already caused untold damage to our trees and forests and to the economy of recreational areas. They point to the fact that it has defoliated two million acres or more annually for the past several years. And they claim that it threatens even worse damage in the future as it spreads into the vast Southern forests. One gloomy official paints a very black picture indeed. "In the years ahead, therefore, we can expect timber losses in excess of thirty-eight million dollars annually, reduced revenues in recreation areas invaded by the pest, destruction of wildlife habitat, reduction of natural beauty and land values, and altered streamflow."

Many others consider that predictions such as this one are highly alarmist, if not ridiculous. They do not dispute the fact that the gypsy caterpillar defoliates large areas of forest from time to time, or that it can be a fearsome nuisance. But how much actual damage, they ask, does the gypsy moth really do?

Aside from a temporary reduction of tourist dollars in recreational areas, many ecologists say that the gypsy moth does very little permanent damage to the environment. Admittedly the tree mortality is highest in new infestations. But if gypsy-moth populations are left alone, these people argue, they will reach a balance with the environment in any area. Everyone can learn to live with

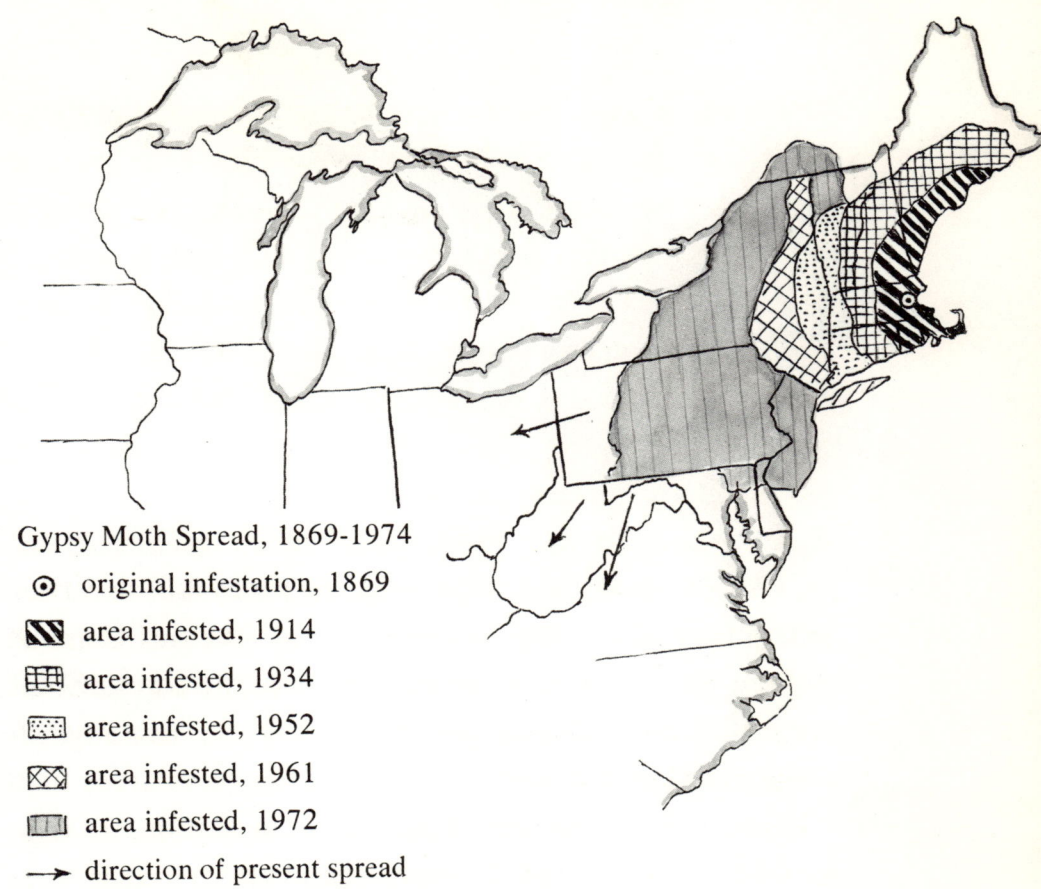

Gypsy Moth Spread, 1869-1974
- ⊙ original infestation, 1869
- area infested, 1914
- area infested, 1934
- area infested, 1952
- area infested, 1961
- area infested, 1972
- → direction of present spread

the gypsy moth, they say, especially if the cost of controlling it proves greater than any damage it does.

Ecologists also point to the fact that the gypsy moth continues to spread, despite all the efforts and funds expended against it. The species widened its range especially quickly after the most determined efforts were made to wipe it out with DDT. In any case, most of the defoliated trees quickly leaf out again, and the woodland suffers little permanent damage.

Two or three successive strippings may kill a certain percentage of the oaks or other trees, but this thinning may in the long run prove beneficial to the forest. Some trees die, but others grow faster after the thinning. A single wind or ice storm may topple far more trees than any killed during a season by gypsy defoliation.

Today the Forest Service acknowledges that fires sometimes benefit the future growth of forests. Perhaps, in the long view, some insect pests of forests may do the same thing.

The Problem

Which of these conflicting viewpoints is the right one? Insects have been attacking man's food crops ever since he began to practice agriculture. They always will. In dealing with such pests, man must consider the damage they do to crops, forests, and animal life and balance this damage against the expense and damage of the control methods used. Control measures are certainly not beneficial if they do more damage than the pests themselves, but there is always the hope that scientists will discover some safe insecticide or biological control that will effectively control the gypsy moth.

Many people, unhappily, think of most insects either with fear or loathing. But that prejudice hardly justifies spending a disproportionate amount of time and money in efforts to control or exterminate them. Some insects are a nuisance or worse. Others are vital to all life, for they pollinate the plants that man and other animals eat.

The gypsy moth has been with us for a long time, and it will be with us longer still. We should attempt to suppress it only when and where it causes more damage than we can easily endure. In many ways, the problem of the gypsy moth is more of a problem to people than to trees and forests.

Appendix:
Insect Pests Often Mistaken for Gypsy Moths

BROWN-TAIL MOTH, *Nygmia phaeorrhoea*
(Northeastern United States and southeastern Canada)

Introduced from Europe to Massachusetts—like the gypsy moth—in the 1890's, the brown-tail moth has white wings. The female, slightly larger than the male, has a wingspread of one and a half inches. The end of her abdomen bears a prominent tuft of brownish hair, which gives the moth its common name. Both sexes are good fliers. After emerging from the cocoon in July, the female mates and lays 300 eggs in a cluster, covering them with brown hairs. The fuzzy brownish caterpillars hatch in two to three weeks and feed in colonies on apple, pear, oak, and many other kinds of trees. When half grown, they overwinter in groups in shelters made of leaves fastened together with silk. When springtime comes, the larvae continue to eat and grow until they reach a length of one and a quarter inches. In June, they pupate for three weeks, then emerge as adult moths.

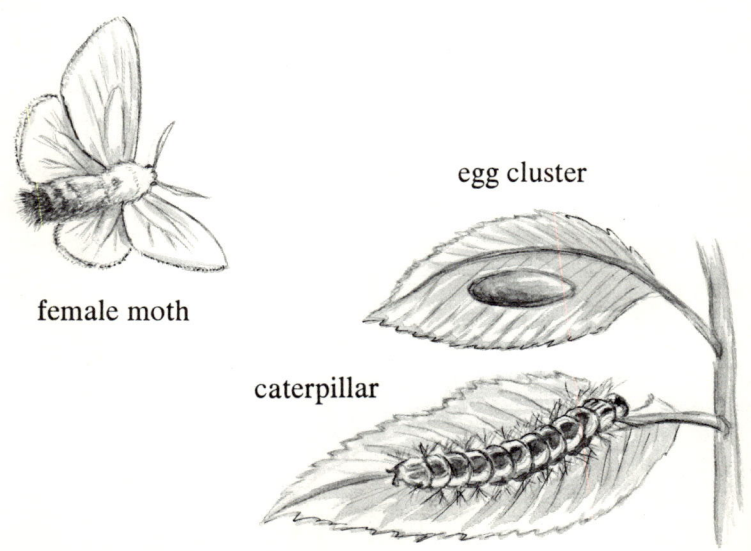

female moth

egg cluster

caterpillar

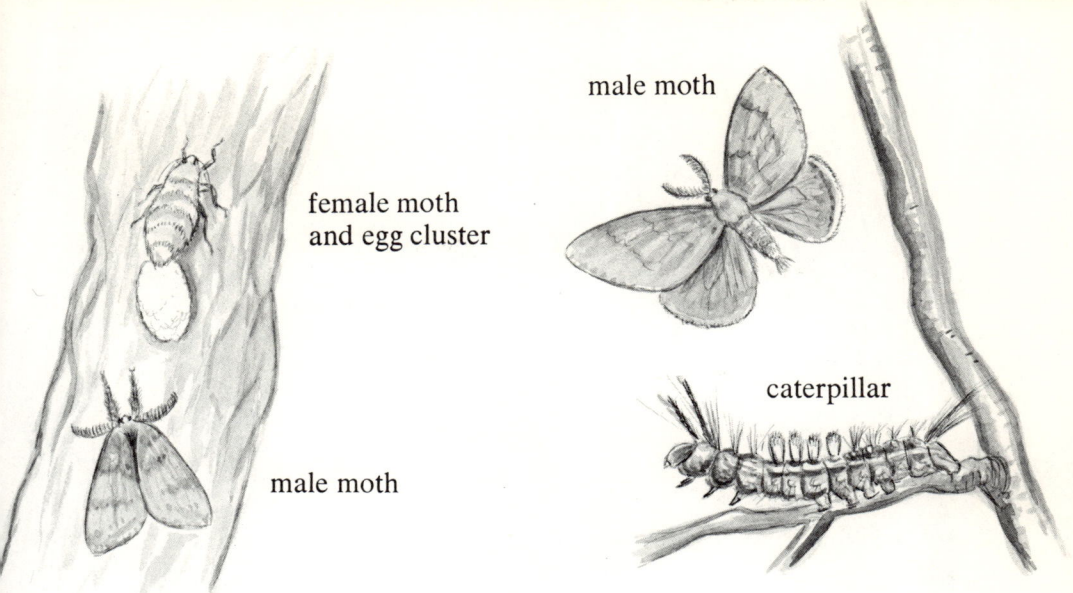

WHITE-MARKED TUSSOCK MOTH, *Hemerocampa leucostigma* (Eastern and Midwestern United States and Southern Canada)

The male moth is gray and white, with a wingspan of one and a half inches. The light-colored female has wing stubs only and cannot fly. In July, after she has emerged from her cocoon and mated, she lays a cluster of 400 to 500 eggs on her cocoon, then covers them with a protective froth. In northern areas, the caterpillars do not hatch until the following spring. The tussock caterpillar is a handsome creature, with a red head and a black stripe down its back bordered on either side with a wide yellow line. It bears four tufts of thick white hair on its back, tufts of white hair on either side, and two long pencils of black hairs over its head and one over its rear end. It eats the leaves of many different kinds of shade and fruit trees. After four to six weeks the larva pupates in a gray-colored cocoon. Adults emerge in ten to fifteen days. In some areas there are two or three generations yearly.

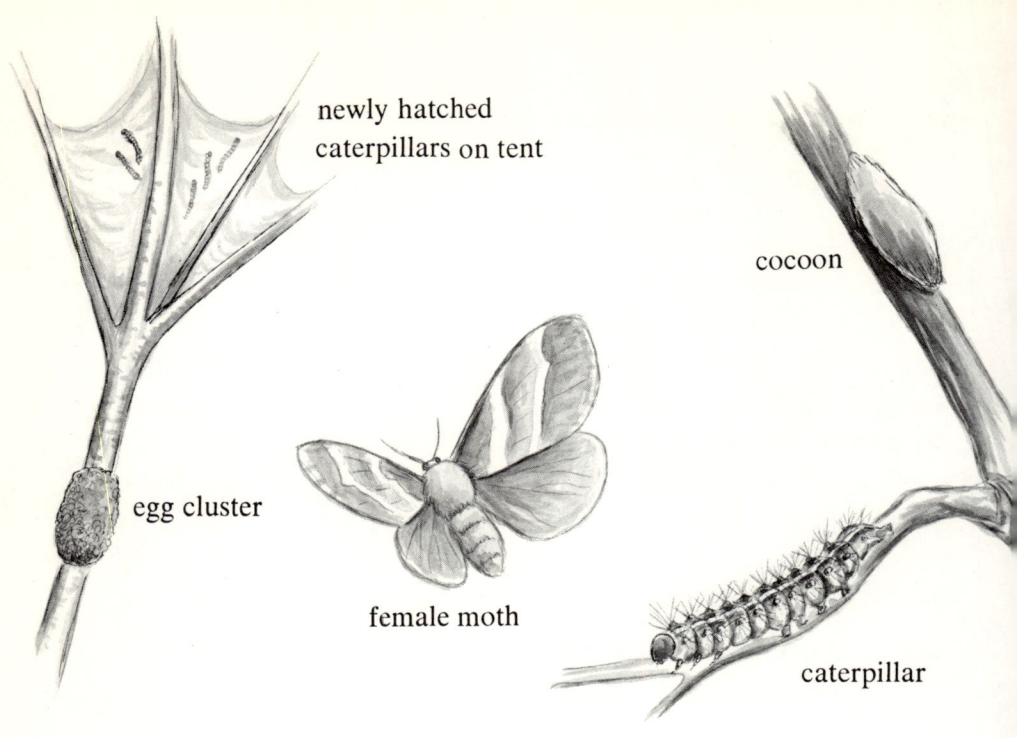

TENT CATERPILLAR, *Malacosoma americanum*
(Eastern United States to Rockies, and Southern Canada)

In early spring newly hatched tent caterpillars spin silvery shelters in the crotches of branches—most often in apple, cherry, or wild cherry trees—as the trees are just beginning to leaf out. The caterpillars come out from their silken tent to feed, then return to the shelter for protection. Full grown by June, the brightly spotted larvae pupate in cocoons for about three weeks before emerging as adult moths. After mating, the female deposits her eggs in rings around twigs, enclosing them in a protective froth that hardens like varnish. In northern areas, the eggs do not hatch out until the following spring. A closely related species, the forest tent caterpillar (*Malacosoma disstria*) attacks forest trees, but makes no tents.

FALL WEBWORM, *Hyphantria cunea*
(most of the United States and Southern Canada

This species is often mistaken for the tent caterpillar, because its caterpillars also spin protective webs. These shelters appear in fall instead of spring, however, and are shaped like bags, enclosing the leaves at the end of a branch instead of being spun in the crotches of branches. The caterpillars feed on almost any kind of trees except conifers. When full grown, they pupate in loose cocoons in the ground, under logs, or in bark crevices. The adult moths have white wings, sometimes with variable dark spots. Emerging in midsummer, the females mate and lay their eggs in masses on leaves.

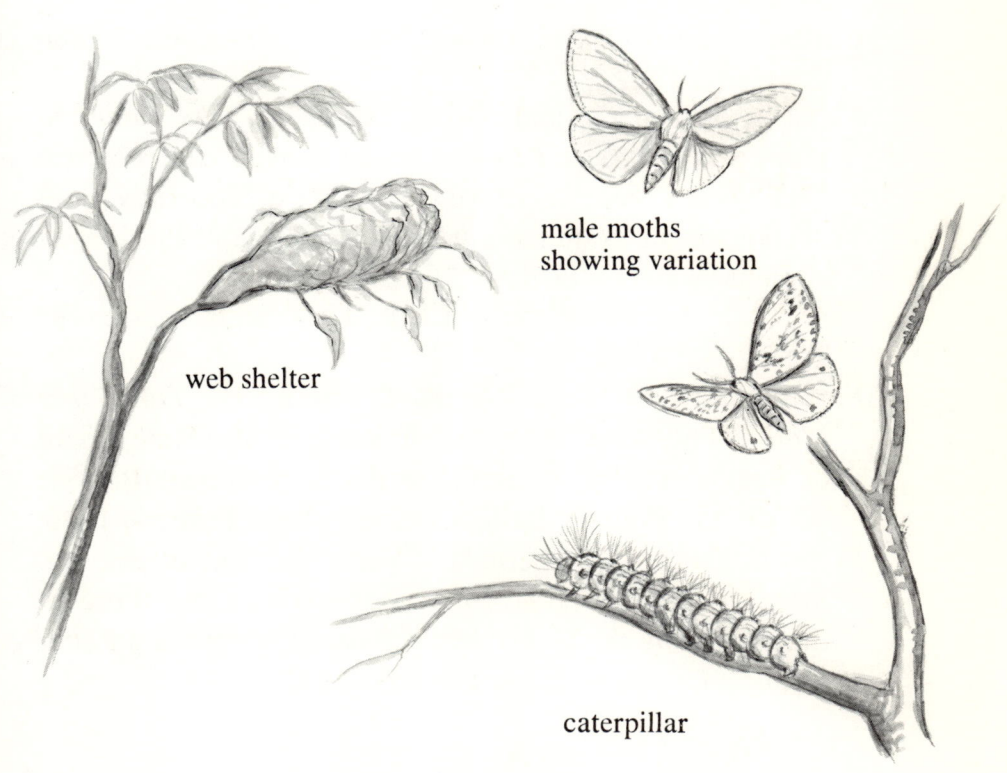

web shelter

male moths showing variation

caterpillar

Further Reading

Barnard, Edward S., "The Scourge of a Moth Named Gypsy." *National Wildlife,* Vol. 11, No. 3, April-May, 1973.

Boehm, George A. W., "After D.D.T., What?" *Technology Review,* July/August, 1972.

Carson, Rachel, *Silent Spring.* Boston: Houghton Mifflin Company, 1962.

Clement, Roland C., and Nisbet, Ian C. T., *The Suburban Woodland: Trees and Insects in the Human Environment.* (Audubon Conservation Report No. 2: a cooperative production of the National Audubon Society and the Massachusetts Audubon Society).

Farb, Peter and the Editors of LIFE, *The Insects.* New York: Time, Inc., 1962.

Forbush, Edward H., and Fernald, Charles H., *The Gypsy Moth.* (Published under the direction of the State Board of Agriculture by Authority of the Legislature). Boston: Wright and Potter Printing Company, State Printers, 1896.

Forbush, Edward H., Fernald, Charles H., and others, *Reports of the State Board of Agriculture on the Work of Exterminating the Gypsy Moth.* Boston: Wright and Potter Printing Company, State Printers, 1892-1903.

Graham, Frank Jr., *Since Silent Spring.* Boston: Houghton Mifflin Company, 1970.

———, "The War Against the Dreaded Gypsies." *Audubon,* Vol. 74, No. 3, May, 1972.

Higdon, Hal, "Well, If Not DDT, Then What?" *The New York Times Magazine,* January 11, 1970.

Kilgore, Wendell W., and Doutt, Richard L., *Pest Control: Biological, Physical, and Selected Chemical Methods.* New York and London: Academic Press, 1967.

Kirkland, A. H., *Annual Reports of the Superintendent for Suppressing the Gypsy and Brown-tail Moths.* Boston: Wright and Potter Printing Company, State Printers, 1906-1908.

Massachusetts Audubon Society, *Man vs. Gypsy Moth.* Lincoln, Massachusetts: Published by the Society.

Rudd, Robert L., *Pesticides and the Living Landscape.* Madison: The University of Wisconsin Press, 1964.

Stefferud, Alfred (Editor), *Insects: The Yearbook of Agriculture, 1952.* Washington, D.C.: The U.S. Government Printing Office.

U.S. Department of Agriculture (Forest Service, and Animal and Plant Health Inspection Service), *Final Environmental Statement of the Cooperative 1973 Gypsy Moth Suppression and Regulatory Program.*

U.S. Department of the Interior (Fish & Wildlife Service), *Fish, Wildlife, and Pesticides.* Washington, D.C.: The U.S. Government Printing Office, 1966.

Wigglesworth, V. B., *The Life of Insects* (A Mentor Book). New York: The New American Library, Inc., 1964.

Worrell, Albert C., "Pests, Pesticides, and People." *American Forests,* July, 1960.

Zwerdling, Daniel, "Birds and Bees." *The New Republic,* October 31, 1970.

Many informational leaflets and other publications on gypsy moths and other insect pests, as well as on pesticides and biological controls, are available from the United States Departments of Agriculture and Interior and may be purchased from the United States Government Printing Office, Washington, D.C. The departments of agriculture or natural resources of many of the states in which the gypsy moth is a threat also furnish informational material upon request. So do many concerned conservation groups besides those mentioned above. Since 1970, The Gypsy Moth Advisory Council has issued for its members a gypsy moth newsletter, edited by Hal Marx, and published at the Northeastern Forest Experiment Station (USDA Forest Service) at 6816 Market Street, Upper Darby, Pennsylvania.

Index

* indicates illustration

Agricultural Research Service (USDA), 78
Agriculture, U.S. Department of, 35, 36, 37, 38, 41-42, 44, 45, 50, 52, 53, 65, 66, 76, 77-78, 79, 81
air age in insect control, 42 *– 48, 43 *, 47 *
Animal and Plant Health Inspection Service (USDA), 78
antennae, 10 *, 11, 65 *
arsenate of lead, 29
arsenic, 25, 29

Bacillus thuringiensis (Bt), 64
Bade, Maria, 69
balance of nature, 57-58
bee, 53 *
beetles, caterpillar-hunting, 35, 62 *
Beroza, Morton, 65

calcium carbonate, 49
carbaryl, *see* Sevin

Carson, Rachel, 50, 57
chemical industry, 50, 52, 53
chemical warfare, early, 29-30 *; *see also* DDT
chickadee, 58 *
control, gypsy moth: bacterial diseases, 63-64; barrier zone, 38, 44; biological (natural), 57-74, 77, 80; chemical, 29-30 *, 40-56, 57, 59, 66; confusion technique, 66; insecticides, 29, 39-56, 55 *, 58-59, 72-73, 80; insect parasites, 34 *, 35-36, 60-62, 61 *; integrated, 78-80; juvenile hormone, 69-71, 72; mechanical methods, 27 *-29, 28 *, 36; predators, 35,· 58 *, 59 *, 60 *, 62 *; quarantine, 36, 80-81; repellants, 28-29, 36, 73-74; selective breeding, 68-69; spraying, 25 *, 26, 29-30 *, 41 *-56, 42 *, 43 *, 47 *, 55 *, 80; sterilization,

93

66-68, 75-76; trapping, 65-66; virus diseases, 62-63
cuckoo, 59 *

DDT, 39, 40-53, 83; harmful effects of, 48-51, 79; Nobel Prize for Chemistry, 41; Trial, 47-48
defoliation, 14, 83, 84 *
Dethier, Vincent, 73
Dexter elm, 27 *
Dipel, 64
Disparlure, 65, 66
downy woodpecker, 58 *

eggs, 12 *-13 *
egg mass (cluster), 12 *, 13 *, 21, 26, 30, 85 *, 86 *, 87 *, 88 *
Entomology, Bureau of (USDA), 35
Entomology Research Division (USDA), 65, 66
Environmental Protection Agency, 52-53, 56
Extension Service (USDA), 78

Fabre, Jean Henri, 65
falcon, 49 *
Fernald, C. H., 24, 25, 31
Fernald, H. T., 24
Fischer, Emil, 40
flies: fruit, 68; screwworm, 67 *, 68; spruce sawfly, 63; tachinid, 61 *, 62

food chain, 48 *
Forest Service (USDA), 42, 78, 79 *, 84
Forbush, Edward H., 25, 34

glands, scent, 10, 45
Gypsy Moth Methods Improvement Laboratory (USDA), 54, 75
Gypsy Moth Trial, *see* DDT Trial

hormones: juvenile, 69-71, 70 *, 72; molting, 69, 70 *
Howard, L. O., 35, 60
hurricane (1938), 39
hydrocarbon, chlorinated, 40, 48, 50, 79

instar, 15
invasion of the U.S., 20-22

Kirkland, A. H., 34, 36
Knipling, Edward E., 66-68

leaves eaten by gpysy caterpillars, 14-15
life cycle, 8 *-18, 9 *, 10 *, 11 *, 12 *, 13 *, 15 *, 16 *, 17 *
linden bug, 71-72

malaria, 41
Massachusetts: Act to Provide for the Suppression of the

Gypsy and Brown-tail Moth, 33-34; Agricultural College, 24; Association for the Suppression of the Gypsy and Brown-tail Moth, 32; Gypsy Moth Commission, 25-26, 30-31, 32; Legislature, 24, 25, 30, 31, 33; Medford, 20, 22-24; *Medford Mercury*, 33; State Board of Agriculture, 25, 31, 32
metamorphosis, 70 *
milky disease, 63, 64
molting, 15 *-16 *, 69-70
moths: brown-tail, 32, 33, 34, 86 *; Cecropia, 71; fall webworm, 89 *; peacock, 65; Polyphemus, 20 *; sphinx, 69; tent caterpillar, 88 *; tobacco hornworm, 69 *; tussock, 52; white-marked tussock, 87 *
mouse, white-footed, 60 *
Mueller, Paul, 41
Murphy, Robert Cushman, 46

National Gypsy Moth Advisory Council, 78
nuthatch, 58 *

outbreaks, gypsy-moth, 18, 19, 37, 61

paper factor, 72, 73
Paris green, 25, 29
pelican, 48 *, 49

penguin, 51 *
pesticide boards, state, 56
phosphates, organic, 40, 53
Plant Pest Control Branch (USDA), 45
population explosion, 18, 22-24
Porthetria dispar, 7, 11, 19
pupa, gypsy moth, 8 *-9, 12, 17 *, 70 *

Quarantine Act (1912), 36

Razzle-Dazzle, 36
Research Service Center (USDA), 77

Science Advisory Committee, 51
Sevin, 52-53, 80
sex lure, 10, 17-18, 45, 64-66
Silent Spring, 50-51, 57
Skylab, 76 *
Sláma, Karel, 71-72
spread, gypsy moth, 32-33 *, 36-39, 38 *, 45, 80-82, 83 *

Tanglefoot, 28
Thuricide, 64
trapping gypsy moths, 44 *-45, 46
Trouvelot, Leopold, 20-22
tubercles, 16*
typhus, 41

virus, polyhedral, 62-63

wasps: braconid, 34 *, 61 *; chalcid, 61 *; ichneumon, 61
Wigglesworth, V. B., 70 *
Williams, Carroll, 71-72

wilt disease, 62-63
World War: First, 36; Second, 39, 41, 42-43

The Author

Robert McClung has been interested in animals of all kinds for as long as he can remember. As a small boy in Butler, Pennsylvania, he became an enthusiastic collector of butterflies and moths, and always kept a few wild pets of one kind or another around the house. In college—he attended Princeton University—he majored in biology.

After college, Mr. McClung became a copywriter for a New York advertising agency, and then served five years on active duty with the Navy during World War II. When the war ended, Mr. McClung's long-standing interest in natural history prompted him to take graduate study in zoology at Cornell. For the next seven years he was on the staff of the Bronx Zoo, first as an assistant in the Animal Departments and then as the zoo's Curator of Mammals and Birds. Later Mr. McClung worked as an editor of natural-history books. He now devotes his full time to writing nature books and illustrating many of them. For his outstanding work he has been named the winner of the 1967 Eva L. Gordon Award for nature literature given by the American Nature Study Society.

Mr. McClung lives in Amherst, Massachusetts, with his wife and two sons. In his spare hours he works for the Amherst Conservation Commission, and in the summer the family goes to Cape Cod.

J632   286252
McCling
Gypsy moth: its history in
America.

Johnson Free Public Library

Hackensack, New Jersey